D1530621

The Managerial Revolution in Higher Education

The Managerial Revolution in Higher Education

by

Francis E. Rourke and Glenn E. Brooks

The Johns Hopkins Press

Baltimore, Maryland 21218
Printed in the United States of America
Library of Congress Catalog Card Number 66–26684

FOREWORD

Some years ago the authors of this book were staff members of the Committee on Government and Higher Education when it undertook a nationwide study of the relations between state government and public institutions of higher education. At that time our investigation centered on the emerging pattern of managerial and fiscal restrictions which various state agencies were beginning to impose on the decisions of college and university officials. In large part this trend toward greater state control reflected uneasiness on the part of governors, legislators, and fiscal and administrative officials over the mounting cost of public higher education. It also showed a deepening conviction on the part of these officials that a greater effort should be made to exercise surveillance over expenditures for higher education. This led to the introduction of a wide range of restraints upon the administration of state colleges and universities—a trend deplored by the committee in its final report.[1]

At the same time, however, it quickly became clear to us in the course of our research that state colleges and universities were themselves beginning to give much more explicit attention to the efficiency of their own internal operations than they had in the past. While resenting the fact that noneducational officials often intervened in the internal affairs of public institutions of higher education, university presidents and other top-level educational administrators were starting to ask many of the same questions about their own institutions that they were being required to answer by budget offices and other state agencies. These questions focused on such matters as cost differentials among academic programs within the institution, the rationale for offering subjects for which there was virtually no student demand, and the possibility of making better use of existing space before launching the construction of new buildings. A shift in managerial perspective of a very dramatic kind was thus taking

[1] The report of the Committee on Government and Higher Education was published as *The Efficiency of Freedom* (Baltimore: The Johns Hopkins Press, 1959). The staff's findings which underlie this report may be found in Malcolm Moos and Francis E. Rourke, *The Campus and the State* (Baltimore: The Johns Hopkins Press, 1959).

place within institutions of higher education as well as in the relations between these institutions and the state.

Of course these two sets of changes were not unrelated to one another. Criticism from state officials itself played an important role in forcing colleges and universities to alter their internal administrative practices. But more was involved here than simply an external stimulus from the environment evoking an internal response from an institution. The truth of the matter is that college and university administration was changing for reasons that were only partially a result of the pressures being exerted from outside. For one thing, new instruments of management were being developed within the university for application to society at large—operations research and systems analysis, for example—and the relevance of these new techniques for university administration gradually became apparent. Moreover, booming enrollments and expanding campuses demanded the use of more refined managerial skills than had ever before been necessary on college campuses.

All these factors working together helped to produce what we have called the "managerial revolution in higher education." It may be argued that we have stretched a point in referring to these managerial changes as a "revolution" since, as we will point out, institutions of higher education still retain much of their traditional style of administration. While we do not deny the force of inertia and tradition in the operation of colleges and universities, as indeed in all organizational systems, we do believe that the pattern of change now taking place in the management of institutions of higher education represents a break sufficiently discontinuous with past practice to merit the description as a revolution. In place of the loose, unstructured, and somewhat casual methods of management practiced in colleges and universities in the past, we have seen a growing commitment to the use of automation in the routine processes of administration, an increased resort to data gathering and research as a basis for policy making, and an expanding effort to develop objective criteria for making decisions on the allocation of resources instead of leaving these matters entirely to the play of campus pressures or the force of tradition. All these developments are traced in considerable detail in the pages that follow. In cumulative effect, these innovations will certainly be regarded by future historians of higher education as giving an entirely new character to university administration.

The changes here described in the management of colleges and universities reflect a trend toward "rationalizing" the management of institutions of higher education. From now on the government of these institutions will reflect a much more conscious effort to plan the course of their development, to relate means to ends, and to seek to obtain a maximum return from the university's resources. To be sure, this attempt can never be more than partially successful, given the intangible goals that institutions of higher education seek and the difficulty of measuring achievement in the pursuits of these goals. But even a partially successful effort in this direction will represent a substantial departure from practices of the past.

While our study thus concentrates on the internal rationalization that is taking place within colleges and universities, we also recognize that there is a growing movement to rationalize the relationships among these institutions of higher education. This movement has taken many forms, but it is primarily reflected in the effort now being made in many parts of the country to establish statewide or interstate systems of higher education in which individual institutions play separate and distinct roles, and in which the system offers comprehensive opportunities for higher education but no single institution is obliged to do so. If the costs of higher education climb still higher, and if the scarcity of talented scholars continues, then we surely can expect to see greater efforts made to rationalize the use of resources by creating such statewide or interstate systems of higher education. Eventually, as the role of the federal government in higher education expands, we may even begin to see the pale outlines of a national system of higher education. This is a trend that will be welcomed by some and resisted by many, but to us it seems inevitable.[2]

The debts we have incurred in the course of this study are formidable ones. We would like to thank the Carnegie Corporation of New York for providing the funds which made our investigation possible, and we acknowledge with special gratitude the assistance of Lloyd Morrisett. We hasten to add, however, that the statements made and the views expressed in this book are solely the responsibility of the authors.

During the three years in which we worked on this study, we were fortunate enough to secure the services of a number of capable and imaginative research assistants. At Johns Hopkins, Matthew Crenson, now at the University of Chicago, did much of the historical research for Chapter 1. Stephen Fraser, presently at San Francisco State College, prepared preliminary material for Appendix C and upon his own initiative developed the analysis of the background of university presidents presented in Appendix B. Max Power returned to Colorado College for a summer between his years at Oxford as a Rhodes Scholar to work with our questionnaire and to do an important part of the research and drafting in our study of space utilization. With skill and precision, Miss Jo Heller

[2] For a recent discussion of such emerging systems of higher education, see James A. Perkins, *The University in Transition* (Princeton, N.J.: Princeton University Press, 1966).

performed the tedious chores of compiling questionnaire data. Peter Bonavich devoted a summer to the statistical analysis of our data and made many valuable contributions before going to Germany on a Fulbright Fellowship. His place was ably filled by Bradley Scharf, who aided in the final stages of revision.

A number of our colleagues across the country made valuable suggestions toward helping us design this project, and, without involving them in responsibility for the finished product, we want to record our gratitude to James Doi, Lyman Glenny, Gilbert and Marcia Johns, Robert McClintock, Robert L. Peabody, Leo Redfern, John Dale Russell, Wilson Smith, Hall Sprague, Arthur Stinchcombe, Robb Taylor, and John Walton.

A portion of the manuscript appeared in somewhat different form in the Administrative Science Quarterly, and we appreciate the willingness of the editors to permit its republication here.

Mrs. Catherine Grover and Mrs. Lois Lentz typed the manuscript through several drafts. Their uncanny accuracy and good sense were among our greatest assets.

Finally, we would like to thank the sources of the data presented in the following chapters. Since our findings are based on an extensive range of interviews and questionnaires, as described in Appendix A, we are heavily in debt to those college and university officials who co-operated with us, either by answering our questionnaire or by allowing us to interview them. The patience of Americans with the unending instrusions of the social scientist seems boundless, and we are happy to pay our tribute to it.

CONTENTS

The Managerial Revolution in Higher Education

Chapter One

BUREAUCRACY IN HIGHER EDUCATION

Universities are the source of constant intellectual and scientific innovation for the society as a whole, and yet, paradoxical as it may seem, university personnel are highly reluctant to accept changes in the operation of the university itself. Only in recent years have American universities shown much inclination to revise their traditional organization and procedure. Even now such changes face heavy opposition. Faculty members who constantly seek to break new ground in their own discipline may steadfastly resist any innovation in university management. Administrative officers themselves often find it difficult to accept departures from the traditional way of doing things. Somehow university personnel, whose lives are devoted to expanding knowledge about the most elusive processes of their environment, nonetheless find it extremely difficult to accept the idea of looking into the campus itself. Yet this resistance to reform cannot simply be written off as lack of vision or a defense of vested interests, for it often is founded upon the belief that higher education could easily be damaged by administrative innovations which might be perfectly acceptable in other types of organizations.

In the context of this conservative tradition, the changes that have recently taken place in the administration of colleges and universities have virtually the appearance of a managerial revolution, for these changes have brought basic modifications in the administrative structure of educational institutions. While the modifications are not yet as thoroughgoing as appearances indicate, they may eventually be as significant for education as they have been in the past for industry and government. In the years since World War II institutions of higher learning have increasingly engaged in a conscious effort to find ways and means of using their resources with greater efficiency. In the course of this attempt to make their operations as rational as possible, a growing number of universities are beginning to experiment with theories and practices identified with what used to be called "scientific management," though now more generally characterized in our day of operations research and systems management as "managerial science."

These managerial innovations are "scientific" at least in the sense that they are characterized by much greater "explicitness, rigor and quantification"[1] than has been the case in the past with academic administration. The new techniques of management include the use of automatic data-processing equipment in the everyday processes of university administration, the operation of professional offices of institutional research, and a growing reliance upon quantitative analysis as a basis for making decisions about the internal allocation of resources in institutions of higher education. The introduction of computer techniques is of particular importance in accelerating this development. While data-processing equipment is most widely used to handle the routine day-to-day chores of university administration, several schools have even begun to program models of their institution on a computer so that top-level administrators may simulate the effects of various policy alternatives before reaching decisions.

Among university administrators the wisdom of applying these new management tools to higher education is being debated vigorously on campuses across the country. Proponents of these administrative innovations feel that more rational techniques—that is, techniques which permit an objective comparison of alternatives in terms of specified goals—give the institution considerably greater efficiency and fairness in its internal operation. They argue that the pressures of growing enrollments, curriculum modernization, and shortages of funds no longer allow an educational institution the luxury of rule-of-thumb procedures. Under a rationalized system of management, inequities in teaching loads, inefficiency in space utilization, or imbalances in salary schedules are clearly revealed to the administrator's view.

It is also claimed that public universities will fare much better in their dealings with state government and the community at large if they rely on space utilization formulas, cost analyses, and other quantitative measuring devices in justifying their requests for support. Advocates of the new science of management believe that resistance to these managerial techniques springs mostly from men who misunderstand the nature of modern administration, or whose positions are threatened by a rational handling of educational resources. Without these management innovations, it is felt, universities will be unable to meet the enrollment surge in the decade to come or to handle the large and complex campus systems now needed in higher education. There is widespread agreement with the proposition that "administration and the administrative process occur in substantially the same generalized form in industrial, commercial, civil,

[1] Edward F. R. Hearle, "How Useful are 'Scientific' Tools of Management?," *Public Administration Review*, Vol. 21 (Autumn, 1961), p. 206.

educational, military, and hospital organizations."[2]

There are others—including men in objective and unthreatened positions —who recall the words of that celebrated critic of academic administration, Thorstein Veblen: "Men dilate on the high necessity of a businesslike organization and control of the university, its equipment, personnel and routine. . . . In this view the university is conceived as a business house dealing in merchantable knowledge, placed under the governing hand of a captain of erudition, whose office it is to turn the means in hand to account in the largest feasible output." This concept of efficiency, said Veblen, "puts a premium on mediocrity and perfunctory work, and brings academic life to revolve about the office of the Keeper of the Tape and Sealing Wax."[3] In more recent and less vitriolic terms, John D. Millett has expressed the belief that "*ideas drawn from business and public administration have only a very limited applicability to colleges and universities.*"[4]

Critics also contend that the impressive procedures of modern management are often little more than camouflage for the prejudices of the administrator. In this sense, some educators fear that a pseudo-science is emerging which will ultimately do violence to higher education as well as to any efforts to develop reliable methods of improving educational administration. This resistance to innovation in management practices is as strong on the administrative as it is on the academic side of campus operations. Registrars, business officers, and other high-ranking administrative personnel may actually constitute the chief source of opposition to the new science of management, mainly because these changes threaten to disturb their own established administrative routines. Faculty members, on the other hand, often appear oblivious to the changes that are taking place—except as the emergence of the IBM card becomes the subject of campus wit. The controversy that has been aroused by the advent of modern management techniques is thus somewhat different from the historic cleavage between faculty and administration in American higher education. In its initial stages, at least, it is primarily a revolution within the structure of university management itself, but a revolution that may eventually have profound significance for faculty and students alike, as incidents in 1964 at the University of California and elsewhere have clearly demonstrated.

[2] Edward H. Litchfield, "Notes on a General Theory of Administration," *Administrative Science Quarterly*, Vol. 1 (June, 1956), p. 28. Litchfield is the former chancellor of the University of Pittsburgh who is widely credited with having introduced the new science of management to that campus.

[3] Thorstein Veblen, *The Higher Learning in America* (New York: American Century Edition, 1957), pp. 62, 76–77.

[4] John D. Millett, *The Academic Community: An Essay on Organization* (New York: McGraw-Hill, 1962), p. 4.

THE EVOLUTION OF UNIVERSITY ADMINISTRATION

In its early development, the administration of colleges and universities in this country was a model of simplicity. There were few administrative tasks to be performed, and no separate caste of administrators was required to undertake these duties. The president managed the university with the assistance of the faculty, subject to over-all direction from a lay board of control. This administrative simplicity was the product in good measure of the small scale of academic operations: enrollments were limited, budgets sparse, and the curriculum quite narrow.

In these early days the college president was chief administrator of the institution in fact as well as in name. Every detail of campus management came under his scrutiny. Moreover, he was able to maintain an active involvement in academic affairs while performing these administrative duties. Very often the president knew each student by name, was familiar with his social and economic background, and had some impression of his intellectual abilities. There was no tendency to look upon the president as the chief executive of a bureaucratic apparatus distinct from the faculty. As a matter of fact students were as likely to encounter the president in the classroom as in his office. McGrath's study of the evolution of college administration revealed that, as late as 1917, over half of all college presidents still retained some teaching responsibilities.[5]

When administrative tasks could not be performed by the president, they were usually taken over by other members of the faculty, a practice still common in European universities. Among the earliest functions to be differentiated in this way were the duties of the librarian and the registrar.[6] As one observer described the pattern of early college administration, "The faculty and the president met weekly and consulted daily; each was familiar with the work of the entire institution; a spirit of cooperation and loyalty naturally prevailed."[7]

Apart from the faculty members themselves, there were few people at an academic institution in earlier days to whom a president might delegate administrative duties. When Henry M. Wriston was a freshman at Wesleyan in 1907 there was not even a dean on campus. A classics professor served as secretary of the faculty, and the college's librarian was

[5] Earl J. McGrath, "The Evolution of Administrative Offices in Institutions of Higher Education in the United States from 1860 to 1933" (unpublished Ph.D. dissertation, University of Chicago, 1938), p. 17.

[6] See in this connection John Dale Russell, "Changing Patterns of Administrative Organization in Higher Education," *Annals* of the American Academy of Political and Social Science, Vol. 301 (September, 1955), pp. 22–31.

[7] J. M. Cattell, *University Control* (New York: The Science Press, 1913), p. 17.

also its bursar, assistant treasurer, and business manager.[8] Moreover, all those who shared responsibility for administering the college's affairs, including the president, depended upon the services of a single stenographer. In 1900 the administrative hierarchy at the University of North Carolina consisted of the president, a registrar, a bursar, a librarian, and a part-time secretary. Students who had occasion to seek advice regarding such matters as a scholarship or the planning of an academic program went directly to the president, who usually referred them to another member of the faculty.[9]

Ultimately this administrative simplicity fell victim to the expanding and changing demands for higher education in this country. The growth in enrollment was itself a factor of principal importance. Around the turn of the century, as the population of colleges and universities began to climb, it became increasingly necessary for specialized officials to handle applications for admission and other aspects of student affairs. The entrance of women into higher education in ever-increasing numbers added to the responsibilities of these officials. With the growth in student body there came an increase in the size of faculties, as well as a vast expansion in the scope of budgets and physical facilities. All these developments further accentuated the need for administrators on college campuses. University presidents could no longer handle by themselves managerial responsibilities as wide-ranging as those they were now asked to undertake.

But it was not only an increase in student population which brought about the growth of bureaucracy on college campuses. Gradually institutions of higher education began to take on new academic functions as well as new students. Following the introduction of the elective system, and with the advent of a more vocationally oriented curriculum, opportunities to choose among a great variety of courses were opened to students, and more elaborate record-keeping systems became necessary to keep track of courses and credit hours. In the course of time colleges and universities also began to assume increased responsibility for the student's social and vocational as well as his intellectual welfare. For example the placement of students in jobs after graduation soon became a routine bureaucratic function. More recently the faculty has begun to slough off certain duties, such as student counseling, which have thereupon become a full-time responsibility for specialized nonteaching personnel.

In the early decades of this century there was one other development

[8] Henry M. Wriston, *Academic Procession: Reflections of a College President* (New York: Columbia University Press, 1959), p. 4.

[9] Louis R. Wilson, *The University of North Carolina, 1900–1930: The Making of a Modern University* (Chapel Hill: University of North Carolina Press, 1957), pp. 4–5.

which helped set the stage for the "managerialized" campus of more recent days. This was the gradual shift in the backgrounds of college presidents. As historians have noted, institutions of higher learning slowly abandoned the tradition of selecting their presidents entirely from the clergy and moved instead to the practice of recruiting them from a variety of secular fields.[10] This shifting pattern of recruitment gave recognition to the fact that the presidential office was now to be regarded as the capstone of an administrative as well as an educational pyramid.

There were some attempts to find relevance for higher education in the tenets of the early scientific management movement launched under the leadership of Frederick W. Taylor at the beginning of this century. In a study undertaken for the Carnegie Corporation one disciple of Taylor, Morris Cooke, urged the application of Taylorist principles to the academic affairs of colleges and universities.[11] Finding, for example, that there were some professors "who literally spent their lives in their laboratories," Cooke came up with the novel suggestion that the faculty be given fixed hours and recreation periods. Taylor himself was aghast to discover "that an institution of such national importance as Harvard should be managed on lines which are almost a century old."[12] By and large, however, the administration of colleges and universities was not much influenced by the old-fashioned Taylorist school of scientific management. Whatever may have been the case at lower levels of the educational system,[13] notions such as time and motion study and the minute supervision of employee performance by so-called functional foremen were plainly irrelevant to a university setting.

It is, however, the period following World War II that has seen the full flowering of managerial change in higher education. The advent of techniques such as operations research and systems analysis, along with the development and widespread application of electronic data-processing equipment for management purposes, has provided college and university officials with an immensely more sophisticated administrative technology than was dreamed of in Taylor's day. At the same time the influx of students and the increasing complexity of college campuses have de-

[10] See in this regard Frederick Rudolph, *The American College and University* (New York: Alfred A. Knopf, 1962), pp. 417–24.

[11] *Academic and Industrial Efficiency* (New York: Carnegie Foundation for the Advancement of Teaching, 1910).

[12] See Henry F. May, *The End of American Innocence* (New York: Alfred A. Knopf, 1959), p. 135.

[13] For an argument that traditional scientific management has penetrated very deeply into vital aspects of elementary and secondary school education, see Raymond E. Callahan, *Education and the Cult of Efficiency* (Chicago: University of Chicago Press, 1962).

manded a good deal more in the way of organized managerial skill than was necessary to run educational institutions in previous eras.

Nothing has been more important in this respect than the growth in the size of university campuses, for our own research clearly shows that managerial innovation is a much more pronounced characteristic of large campuses than it is of small ones.[14] Table 1–1 points up the fact that the large campus has become the dominant environment in public higher education today.

TABLE 1–1: ENROLLMENT, STATE COLLEGES AND UNIVERSITIES, 1954/55–1964/65

	Under 2,000		2,000–5,000		5,000–10,000		Over 10,000	
	No. of Insti- tutions	%[a]	No. of Insti- tutions	%	No. of Insti- tutions	%	No. of Insti- tutions	%
1954/55	235	20.3	68	22.9	32	24.3	18	32.5
1964/65	107	5.6	133	19.3	58	19.5	59	55.6

[a] The percentage figures in this table represent the proportion of the total student body across the country which is enrolled in each size category of institution.

In short it has been the conjunction of two events—the development of a more advanced administrative technology and the emergence of a large campus setting conducive to the application of more refined administrative skills—that has paved the way for the managerial innovations taking place in higher education today.

Moreover, pressure from the external environment, so often in the past a source of change in colleges and universities, has given considerable impetus to these managerial developments. Governors, state legislatures, and other groups interested in obtaining a maximum return on the educational dollar have been a vital factor in building support for a more efficient system of campus operations in public higher education. In a number of states, co-ordinating agencies in the field of higher education have exerted strong pressure in the same direction. These administrative and political forces in the immediate environment have added to the pressure for new patterns of organization and management in public colleges and universities.

Equally important has been the influence of the federal government. As recent years have seen a steady growth in the funds channeled by

[14] In this regard see Appendix B. The data also show a marked tendency for institutions in the western part of the United States to be more receptive to managerial innovation than are schools in other parts of the country.

national agencies into colleges and universities (private as well as public), institutions of higher education have been increasingly faced with the necessity of justifying requests for federal financial support, or accounting for funds already expended. This has pushed them in the direction of much more elaborate systems of record keeping, as well as toward more explicit analyses of costs and clearer definitions and descriptions of institutional goals and procedures. In essence, therefore, federal aid has had a bureaucratizing effect on university operations: "administration becomes a much larger aspect of the total university enterprise."[15]

Some federal agencies find it much more convenient to deal with a single source of decision in their contacts with universities rather than with a variety of departments with varying standards. This has had a centralizing effect upon university administration. At the same time, however, grants by other agencies to individual departments and faculty members may reinforce their autonomy and make it more difficult to bring them under effective overhead supervision. Hence, while federal aid may not, as was often prophesied in the past, bring federal control, there is no doubt that it is increasing the work load and changing some procedures in university administration.[16]

RESISTANCE TO ADMINISTRATIVE RATIONALIZATION

Opposition from administrators and faculty members to the new forms of management is rooted in certain basic beliefs regarding both the administrative and the educational processes that have long been prevalent in colleges and universities in this country. These beliefs are (1) that educational outputs cannot be measured, and that any attempt to do so is ludicrous if not actually subversive of the purposes for which academic institutions exist; (2) that there is an inherent conflict between administrative efficiency on the one hand and academic effectiveness on the other; (3) that efforts to improve management efficiency are really designed to increase the power of administrators at the expense of faculty members. Each of these assumptions is subject to separate examination in the discussion that follows.

Measurement in Higher Education

The belief that educational outputs cannot be measured is a highly cherished one in higher education and it is, in some respects at least,

[15] Clark Kerr, *The Uses of the University* (Cambridge: Harvard University Press, 1963), p. 67.

[16] Some of the conflicting effects of federal aid upon university administration are explored in Homer D. Babbidge, Jr., and Robert M. Rosenzweig, *The Federal Interest in Higher Education* (New York: McGraw-Hill, 1962), pp. 117–26.

unassailable. As is the case with all organizations that produce intangible products and employ a large number of highly skilled professional staff members to achieve their goals, the output of institutions of higher education does not readily lend itself to quantitative measurement. Judgments about many aspects of institutional productivity must ultimately be based on qualitative rather than quantitative standards of achievement and, in the absence of agreed-upon objective criteria, must ultimately be highly subjective in character.

It would be foolish, however, to refuse to accept any use of quantitative techniques in the management of colleges and universities. There are many aspects of administrative performance which are as measurable in institutions of higher education as they are in any other organization—the cost of taking care of buildings and grounds, for example. Furthermore, the area of academic performance itself is not altogether immune from quantitative assessment. While it may not, for example, be possible to compare in any significant way the performance of a chemistry and a classics department, it may be possible to rate the achievements of a single chemistry department against those of similar departments elsewhere. At the very least, subjective comparisons can be made between the standing of a university department within its professional discipline at one period of its history with its position at another.

The truth of the matter is that the academic community has traditionally made much more use of quantitative criteria in making judgments on educational policy than it has usually been prepared either to recognize or acknowledge. Very often, however, this reliance upon factual data is not made explicit but is more or less "smuggled" into the decision-making process. As a result quantitative data may actually exercise much more influence than would be the case if the facts were brought into the open where they could be subjected to critical scrutiny. For example some deans who would stoutly deny that their decisions are made on a quantitative basis will actually be found, upon close inspection, to be leaning upon highly subjective and often erroneous factual assumptions in framing university policy.

Of course the introduction of quantitative measurement into the field of educational policy has its own pitfalls. There is always the danger, to which all organizations are subject, that quantitative standards will tend to drive out qualitative criteria altogether. Robert Roy points out: "Numbers always tend to dominate administrative decisions, even when such numbers as are available are grossly inaccurate or inadequate."[17]

[17] Robert H. Roy, *The Administrative Process* (Baltimore: The Johns Hopkins Press, 1958), p. 85.

An illustration Roy singles out is a familiar one on the academic landscape—the practice of appraising a faculty member in terms of the length rather than the quality of his bibliography. Given the difficulty of making comparisons in terms of quality, it is easy to see why academic administrators should give quantitative criteria greater weight than they really deserve. However spurious the appearance of precision may be, numerical measurements have the air of certainty for which all executives yearn in making decisions. But excessive reliance upon quantitative criteria in any institution with purposes as intangible as education is the most foolhardy kind of administrative delusion.

It is also necessary to recognize that the successful use of quantitative criteria in some aspects of decision making does not warrant their application to other areas of policy for which they are fundamentally unsuited. Operations research, for example, has won great renown as a method of studying the management of all organizations as quantitatively as possible with the end in view of improving their performance. Yet it has severe limitations when it is applied to complex problems, as noted by Charles Hitch, who was one of the chief practitioners of this new approach to management while serving as Controller of the Department of Defense:

> I would make the empirical generalization from my experience at RAND and elsewhere that operations research is the art of sub-optimizing, i.e. of solving some lower-level problems, and that difficulties increase and our special competence diminishes by an order of magnitude with every level of decision making we attempt to ascend. The sort of simple explicit model which operations researchers are so proficient in using can certainly reflect most of the significant factors influencing traffic control on the George Washington Bridge, but the proportion of the relevant reality which we can represent by any such model or models in studying, say, a major foreign policy decision, appears to be almost trivial.[18]

In the final analysis, therefore, it should be very clearly kept in mind that the relevance of quantitative methods of management to some kinds of university decisions does not justify their application to all areas of academic life. At the same time, the inapplicability of quantitative methods to some areas of educational policy does not warrant their exclusion from all spheres of academic administration. The successful management of universities today depends upon a recognition of this distinction.

Efficiency and Effectiveness

The distinction between efficiency and effectiveness is a familiar one in the literature of administration. The efficiency of any organization can be

[18] As quoted by Charles E. Lindblom, "The Science of 'Muddling Through,'" *Public Administration Review*, Vol. 19 (Spring, 1959), p. 80. Interestingly enough, Hitch has since moved into university administration.

defined in terms of its capacity to achieve results with a given expenditure of resources—in short, the ratio between organizational inputs and outputs. Effectiveness, on the other hand, may be said to refer to the degree of success an organization enjoys in doing whatever it is trying to do. Insofar as it can be measured at all (and this is exceedingly difficult with organizations like universities that produce no readily quantifiable product), the effectiveness of an organization is reflected by its standing or achievements as compared with other organizations of its type.[19]

Obviously, efficiency and effectiveness bear a close relation to each other, since an organization's effectiveness may well depend on the careful use of its limited resources. But it is equally clear that the two may not necessarily coincide, and that an organization's efforts to husband its resources may seriously limit its effectiveness. As a general rule university administrators, particularly on the business side of campus operations, tend to be oriented toward the criterion of efficiency, while the faculty usually repairs to the standard of effectiveness. Many of the disputes that break out on college campuses between administrators and professors are in fact built around this dichotomy.

One observer of the development of techniques of scientific management in the administration of colleges and universities wrote somewhat caustically to the authors of this study that "the quality of undergraduate education at any institution will vary inversely with the 'evidences' of scientific management to be found on campus." This attitude is not uncommon.[20] It mirrors a widespread belief among academicians that the ideal educational environment is one which affords the maximum opportunity for creativity and spontaniety—conditions which administration, by its insistence upon regularity and routine, does not encourage. As compared with other organizational systems, higher education in this country has always been disorderly and undisciplined, and there are many educators who devoutly believe that academic creativity and inspiration wither in an atmosphere of stringent administration.[21] There are certainly many

[19] This distinction between efficiency and effectiveness follows that presented by Amitai Etzioni in *Modern Organizations* (Englewood Cliffs, N.J.: Prentice-Hall, 1964), pp. 8–10. There are, however, other ways in which such a distinction may be drawn. See, for example, Chester I. Barnard, *The Functions of the Executive* (Cambridge: Harvard University Press, 1938), pp. 55–61.

[20] Our study found no tendency for institutions of the first rank to turn their backs on new managerial techniques. Many of the outstanding academic institutions in this country have been at the forefront of managerial change.

[21] No one has more forcefully expressed this view in modern times than Paul Goodman: "I am proposing simply to take teaching-and-learning in its own terms, for the students and teachers to associate in the traditional way and according to their existing interest, but *entirely dispensing with the external control, administration, bureaucratic machinery, and other excrescences that have swamped our communities of scholars.*"

students who feel this way, as is evident from the swelling chorus of undergraduate complaints against the computerized campus.

One of the salient problems here is the fact that educational inputs—in the form of resources such as money and personnel—can be subjected to a substantial degree of measurement, while educational outputs—in the form of educated students and new knowledge—tend to be resistant to this approach. No institution can be certain what sort of students it is turning out, much less what may be the quality of its faculty's research. Institutions often wind up competing for the reputation rather than the reality of quality—to be known as a good place rather than to be a good place. Every attempt to rank institutions of higher education in terms of quality is seriously vitiated by the difficulty of developing a valid measure of educational outputs.

But the fact that educational inputs are more measurable than educational outputs opens up the possibility that efficiency rather than effectiveness may often become the dominant orientation of university management. Moreover, since efficiency itself is the ratio between inputs and outputs, and since the input side of the efficiency ratio is usually more measurable than output, the task of increasing efficiency may soon come to be identified by many administrators with reductions in input. In this way the goal of efficiency can be translated into the goal of cutting costs and saving money. As has been pointed out regarding attempts to introduce "efficiency" in elementary and secondary school education, "the record shows that the emphasis was not at all on 'producing the finest product' but on the 'lowest cost.' In all the efforts which were made to demonstrate efficiency, it was not evidence of the excellence of the 'product' which was presented, but data on per-pupil costs."[22] Perhaps the best safeguard against tendencies of this sort is the development of better avenues of studying output, so as to enable administrators to keep in focus the possibility of improving the efficiency ratio by increasing output as well as by reducing costs.

Administrators and Professionals

From the perspective of organization theory, at least, institutions of higher education belong in the category of professional organizations, along with hospitals, laboratories, and scientific institutes and agencies.

The Community of Scholars (New York: Random House, 1962), p. 168. Or, as Abraham Flexner put it many years ago, "Efficiency in administration and fertility in the realm of ideas have in fact nothing to do with each other—except, perhaps, to hamper and destroy each other." *Universities, American, English, German* (New York: Oxford University Press, 1930, p. 186.

[22] See Callahan, *Education and the Cult of Efficiency*, p. 244.

That is to say, they are institutions whose staff includes a sizable percentage of highly trained employees in the form of faculty members who strongly identify with the skill they practice rather than the institution to which they are attached. [23] In the more prestigious colleges and universities the professional academic staff dominates the decision-making process with respect to such vital matters as the selection of faculty members and the determination of educational programs.

Like all bureaucratic systems, professional organizations face the continuing probem of maintaining themselves in existence as institutions. In the case of colleges and universities, for example, there are certain routine housekeeping chores which need to be performed on a day-to-day basis. Records must be kept, buildings and grounds maintained, and the students fed and housed. In addition an educational organization, like other institutions, can survive only by maintaining an adequate flow of revenues into its treasury. In the United States the performance of these varied tasks has required the presence on campus of a variety and a growing number of administrative staff members. These administrators do not perform the central educational services for which colleges and universities are created. They do not, for example, ordinarily teach or carry on research. But their presence is indispensable if the institutions in which faculty members do carry on these activities are to be kept in daily operation.

Needless to say, the relationship between administrators and professionals is not always an easy one in institutions of higher education. Authority relationships in particular are far from clear. While the faculty may have jurisdiction over educational decision making, it is administrators who control the disposition of financial and other resources upon which decisions on academic policy ultimately depend. In this competitive context, proposals to rationalize the management of institutions of higher education can easily be interpreted as a conspiracy to augment the power of administrators at the expense of faculty members. At the larger and more prestigious schools it has been necessary, traditionally, for management innovations to be introduced with considerable diplomatic finesse to allay the suspicion of faculty members that all such changes portend some undesirable increase in administrative power.

Of course there are campuses, particularly those with a teachers' college tradition, where the pre-eminence of administrators is firmly established.

[23] For a revealing analysis of the distinctive characteristics of professional organizations, see Amitai Etzioni, "Authority Structure and Organizational Effectiveness," *Administrative Science Quarterly*, Vol. 4 (June, 1959), pp. 43–67. See also Francis E. Rourke, "Bureaucracy in Conflict: Administrators and Professionals," *Ethics*, LXX (April, 1960), 220–27.

At such institutions the introduction of new management techniques can proceed as far and as fast as the administrators' sophistication about such techniques permits. However, virtually all these institutions are anxious to improve their academic standing, and every step they take in the direction of upgrading themselves in the academic hierarchy will inevitably make it more difficult for administrators to govern in this untrammeled way. A dramatic illustration of this fact recently occurred at one state college in the East, where the president—in his eagerness to move his institution from a teacher-training to a liberal arts orientation—recruited a substantial number of young and professionally oriented faculty members to his campus. Within the short space of two years, this avant-garde group was the source of a faculty revolt against the president's autocratic managerial methods, which eventually led to his resignation. In this case the president's desire for increased academic status proved to be the direct cause of his own administrative downfall.

The tension between administrators and professionals will long remain part of the setting that conditions the reception accorded managerial change in higher education. It may well be that the stress between these two cultures in the academic community will diminish if higher education continues to grow in affluence over the next decade. In the past much of this tension has been generated by the fact that institutions of higher education operated in an economy of poverty—in power as well as other resources. Any expansion in the role of administrators always seemed to require a corresponding reduction in the influence of faculty members. Academic staff and administration were in effect playing a zero-sum game in which the gains for one side had to be offset by losses for the other.

Now, however, the situation is greatly changed. With booming enrollments and the growing demand for technical skills generated by automation, new opportunities have been opened up for colleges and universities to play an expanding role in the nation's economic life. As a result there has been power enough to go around at a great many institutions. Faculty and administration are, in effect, now playing a non-zero-sum game. Each side has the opportunity to increase its winnings without decreasing the total available to the other. Thus we see on many campuses today an unprecedented proliferation of administrative offices and functions. Central services such as guidance and counseling are expanding in every direction and a clutch of vice-presidents and other administrators have moved into the educational hierarchy. In short, the administration of colleges and universities has become a major growth industry.

At the same time, however, the horizons of faculty members have been expanding at an even more rapid rate, as competition for academic talent has sent salaries ever higher. Some academic departments have acquired such substantial sources of outside support that they virtually spin themselves off from the university budget. Professors are now subject to heavy attack for deserting their students in their quest for greener pastures.[24] To be sure these trends can easily be exaggerated. The monetary benefits of the space-age prosperity for higher education have not been equally distributed among all disciplines or institutions. There are still many pockets of poverty in higher education. But recent developments have clearly demonstrated that, contrary to traditional expectations, it is possible for administrative and faculty power to grow simultaneously—in a complementary rather than a competitive way.

Signs of unrest on college campuses suggest that the casualties of this non-zero-sum game between faculty and administrators may well be the undergraduate students, suffering under what they regard as the double indignity of impersonal treatment by computerized administrators and desertion of teaching responsibilities by the faculty. Clark Kerr, president of the University of California, has described the problem in these terms: "The students find themselves under a blanket of impersonal rules for admissions, for scholarships, for examinations, for degrees. . . . If the faculty looks on itself as a guild, the undergraduate students are coming to look upon themselves more as a 'class'; some may even feel like a 'lumpen proletariat.' Lack of faculty concern for teaching, endless rules and requirements, and impersonality are the inciting causes."[25] It is not the least of the ironies of the recent history of higher education that the outbreak of student riots on the Berkeley campus in the fall of 1964 should make Kerr the first victim of the malady he had so aptly diagnosed.

THE SCOPE OF THIS STUDY

This study of managerial innovation in higher education was launched with two principal objectives in view. The first was that of gauging the extent to which new techniques of management have actually permeated American higher education. How widespread has been the movement toward more rationalized administration in the colleges and universities of this country? As noted earlier, several areas of managerial activity were singled out for systematic examination in this connection, including the use of electronic data-processing equipment in academic administration, the establishment of offices of institutional research, and the development of methods for making more rational decisions about the allocation of basic organizational resources within higher education, both in budgeting

[24] See, for example, John Fischer, "Is There a Teacher on the Faculty?," *Harper's Magazine*, Vol. 230, No. 1377 (February, 1965), pp. 18–28.

[25] Kerr, *The Uses of the University*, pp. 103–4.

and the use of physical facilities. In addition we have attempted to trace changes in the character and operation of top-level university administration which both reflect and contribute to the managerial revolution now taking place in higher education.

Our second objective has been that of measuring—in a preliminary way at least—what impact the new science of management has had upon the academic community. At the root of concern in this respect have been two basic questions: (1) Are colleges and universities making different kinds of decisions from those they once did as a result of the new management techniques available to them? (2) Have the innovations in management brought important shifts in control over decision making in colleges and universities in this country? In short, has the revolution in management effected major changes either in the character of educational policy or in the groups participating in its development? Or, in C. P. Snow's phrase, are there new men of power in higher education who have brought a new style of managerial decision to the ivory tower?

The methods followed in gathering data for this study are described in some detail in Appendix A. Basically we relied on both a questionnaire—sent to over 400 institutions across the country—and upon interviews conducted with over 200 individuals at 33 colleges and universities in 16 states.[26] Included among our interviews were a number of talks with officials having statewide jurisdiction over several institutions of higher learning, as well as administrators with regional or national responsibilities in the field of higher education. The four-part questionnaire covered the topics of institutional research, the use of electronic data-processing equipment, budgeting, and space allocation.[27]

Both the sample of institutions at which interviews were conducted and the list of schools to which questionnaires were addressed focus on the public sector of higher education. This emphasis is based on the fact that one of the chief aims of this study was to trace the influence of the new managerial developments upon the traditionally autonomous position of public colleges and universities as agencies of the state—an autonomy many educators believe has been seriously undermined in recent years.[28] The question of whether these techniques of management make public institutions of higher education more or less vulnerable to outside control was a major concern in this investigation from the outset.

[26] The institutions in the sample are listed in Appendix A.

[27] These questionnaires may be found in Appendix B. The list of schools to which they were sent was drawn from the U.S. Office of Education, *Education Directory*, 1963–64, Part 3 (Washington: U.S. Government Printing Office, 1964).

[28] In this regard, see the report of the Committee on Government and Higher Education, *The Efficiency of Freedom*, and Moos and Rourke, *The Campus and the State*.

But it was also clear to us from our research that private universities can be as heavily influenced in their internal administrative development by the onset of the new managerial science as are public institutions. In some cases, in fact, private institutions may be pace setters in the field of managerial innovation. Massachusetts Institute of Technology, for example, has pioneered in the use of computers for class scheduling. We thus sent questionnaries to a number of private as well as public institutions. The results of our research led us to the belief that public institutions differ from private schools chiefly with respect to the outside influences and controls to which they are subject. (Although, with the advent of programs of federal assistance to private universities, this difference appears to be narrowing.) As far as purely internal administrative problems and practices are concerned, we are convinced that the two types of institutions are virtually indistinguishable and that our findings in this regard are as applicable to private as they are to public colleges and universities.

In Chapter 2 this survey of the managerial revolution in higher education begins with a look at the role which computers have come to play in the operation of colleges and universities. Computers are at the center of the new science of management, partly because they serve as a symbol of managerial change, but also because computer technology has made possible many of the other innovations that have taken place in such areas as institutional research and resource allocation. Certainly no aspect of managerial change in higher education has received more publicity than the use of automatic data-processing equipment. Much of this publicity is unfavorable, reflecting the belief that the computer is the source of impersonality in higher education today. Understandably enough, a good many people look back with nostalgia upon the simpler campus of yesterday, with Mark Hopkins on one end of the log and the student on the other. But in this day of vast and complex educational institutions, the ironic possibility does exist that only the computer may have the capacity to deal with each student in terms of his unique characteristics.

Chapter Two

THE COMPUTERIZED CAMPUS

During the student riots on the Berkeley campus in 1964, it was reported, some of the demonstrating students were marching around the campus with signs which bore the legend, "I am a student. Please do not fold, spindle, or mutilate." In the Midwest a determined group of faculty members attempted to sabotage a newly installed computer system for recording grades by punching random holes in the cards used to report grades to the IBM machine. At yet another university an embattled registrar fought a proposal to introduce a streamlined computer registration system, arguing that his office could do the job more efficiently with traditional hand methods. Whether these reactions are justified or not, they serve as a reminder that institutions of higher education have begun to convert important segments of their administrative procedure to electronic computers and that the effects of this conversion are being felt in all quarters of the academic community.

Three key findings have emerged from our own survey of computer use in university administration.[1] First, the potential of computers in this area is still largely unrealized; a new world of computer management and control lies ahead in higher education. Up to this point, at least, computers are still being used mainly to increase the speed, accuracy, and general effectiveness of many routine administrative operations in state universities. But the modern electronic computer has a capacity for highly sophisticated varieties of administrative analysis which go far beyond such routine clerical concerns.[2] As mentioned earlier, computer science has reached a point at which mathematical models of universities can be programed on computers so that complex policy decisions can be tested

[1] For the questionnaire used in this survey see Appendix B.

[2] The distinction between computers and other forms of calculating equipment is often blurred. The General Electric Company defines a computer specifically as "a stored-program digital computer capable of performing sequences of internally-stored instructions, as opposed to calculators on which the sequence is impressed manually (desk calculator) or from tape or cards (card programmed calculator)." *Glossary of Computer Terminology*, (Phoenix, Ariz.: Computer Department, General Electric Company, n.d.), p. 6.

on the model before they are put into effect. Moreover, computer-based administrative games, resembling the war games of the Pentagon, have been developed for the training of university administrators. As a central element in what Herbert Simon has called "the new science of management decision,"[3] computers may thus explore new paths to problem solving which reach far beyond the ability of the human mind.

Secondly, new designs for administrative organization have appeared along with the introduction of computers, and these new concepts may be of paramount importance in the long run. Bold plans for integrated information management systems have been developed around the computer. In the past the sheer complexity of operations led to a compartmentalization of administrative activities in large organizations. The computer, on the other hand, holds out promise of a comprehensive integration of information which will permit organizational unification. Administrators have therefore begun to think of the university as a single organizational system, rather than in terms of arbitrarily separated administrative units, and to devise procedures which cut across many of the old jurisdictional boundaries. In this process the computer and the men who operate it have been moved into positions of new prominence in the administrative hierarchy.

Finally, the evidence thus far available suggests that the introduction of computers frequently influences the distribution of authority and the shape of policy within an academic institution. In this reshaping of authority and policy, critically important side-effects may appear in the form of student alienation, faculty unrest, or intra-administrative struggles. If these side-effects are not anticipated or remedied they may negate many of the expected gains to be made from a shift to computer operations. Although most computer work is performed in the name of administrative efficiency alone, the fact of the matter is that computers are sometimes used by skilled administrators to accomplish program changes of considerable importance within an institution. For example, in converting to a computer processing system for student admissions, the administrator may at the same time change the admissions criteria on the grounds that certain standards cannot be readily programed on the computer. But on campuses already uneasy about impersonal, mass-produced education, the use of computers to change patterns of power and policy involves a high degree of risk, since their use may trigger intense reactions among the affected parties, who then flail the computer as a symbol of dehumanized education.

Yet while the computer is easily the most dramatic symbol of the "new

[3] Herbert Simon, *The New Science of Management Decision* (New York: Harper and Row, 1960).

science" in university management, it is not necessarily the spearhead of administrative innovation. Techniques of scientific management were cultivated in the United States long before the appearance of electronic computers, and on many university campuses the computer was preceded by other devices and agencies commonly associated with the new managerial science. At the University of Minnesota, for example, advanced institutional research employing complex quantitative data had been a going concern for several decades before the arrival of computers. Other institutions had developed highly rationalized budgetary formulas, as well as space-planning and utilization procedures, well in advance of the electronic computer. But the computer has given new impetus to other elements of modern management and has clearly become a major new factor in bringing on administrative innovation in American higher education.

AREAS OF COMPUTER APPLICATION

As in business and industry, the swiftness of the introduction of electronic computers in higher education has been breathtaking. According to one authority, "there were less than five university computer installations at the beginning of 1956, about a dozen when 1957 began, and over sixty installed or planned at the start of 1958."[4] By 1964 the total number of computer systems in institutions of higher education, both public and private, had grown to an estimated five hundred, with more being planned every day.[5] An increasingly large number of computers are being programed for administrative work. The returns from our questionnaire indicated that 53 per cent of all state institutions of higher education were using computers for administrative purposes.[6] Many other state colleges and universities were operating computers but so far have confined them to research work.

The administration of student affairs is the dominant area of computer use in state colleges and universities. Financial affairs occupy second place, followed by physical plant management. General policy planning is a growing field of computer application which depends upon the availability of information from other areas of university administration. But so far the computers are still being used most heavily in the day-to-day

[4] John A. Postley, *Computers and People: Business Activity in the New World of Data Processing* (New York: McGraw-Hill, 1960), p. 21.

[5] This estimate is based on various surveys made by computer companies and the American Association of Collegiate Registrars and Admissions Officers.

[6] In a comparative check of municipal and private institutions we also found that 58 per cent of the municipal institutions and 56 per cent of the private institutions reported that they used computers for administrative work.

administrative routines of higher education. These rankings of administrative use, as spelled out in Tables 2–1 and 2–2, are based on the reports of state colleges and universities that have a central computer facility and are in a position to make comparisons of the time and number of programs employed in different administrative areas. Institutions without a central facility, but with computers located in various university offices, follow roughly the same pattern of computer use.[7]

[7] Our generalizations are necessarily based on rather arbitrary categories of administration, since universities vary extensively in the terminology they use to describe their administrative activities. E. P. Miles, Jr., and D. L. Hartford, in their earlier survey, *A Study of Administrative Uses of Computers in Colleges and Universities of the United States* (Tallahassee: Florida State University, 1962), worked out rankings on the basis of the number of institutions using computers for specified purposes. In our survey we sought information about time consumed as well as total number of institutions using computers in a particular application. In the two measures the first and second rankings are the same, while the third and fourth rankings trade positions.

TABLE 2–1: COMPUTER USE IN ADMINISTRATION OF STATE UNIVERSITIES AND COLLEGES

Administrative Activity	No. of Schools	% of Total (n = 134)[a]
Student affairs	130	97
Financial administration	119	89
Policy planning	93	69
Physical plant management	88	66

[a] Responding to our questionnaire on computers (see Appendix B) were 134 state schools with central computer agencies.

TABLE 2–2: RANKING OF TIME SPENT ON COMPUTERS BY MAJOR ADMINISTRATIVE ACTIVITY

Ranking[a] (by time consumed)	Major Administrative Activity[b]			
	Student Affairs	Financial Administration	Physical Plant Management	Policy Planning
1	65	35	0	0
2	33	42	6	7
3	2	7	29	21
4	0	5	18	23

[a] Institutions were asked to rank the activities listed, 1, 2, 3, and 4, in terms of the amount of time they pre-empted on the computer.

[b] These figures are percentages and are based on 134 state schools with central computer agencies.

Student Affairs

Because of the heavy pressures of growing enrollments the computer has been pressed into the service of the registrar, the admissions officer, and other officials responsible for the management of student affairs. The results have been highly controversial, for it is in this area more than any other that the charge is heard that universities have mechanized and depersonalized the educational process.

TABLE 2–3: USE OF COMPUTERS BY STATE COLLEGES AND UNIVERSITIES IN ADMINISTRATION OF STUDENT AFFAIRS

	Present Use		Future Use [a]	
Activity	No. of Schools (1)	% of Total (n = 134) (2)	No. of Schools (3)	% Increase [b] (4)
Registration	122	91	24	20
Grading records	119	89	12	10
General student records	109	81	24	22
Admissions	74	55	34	46
Testing	8	6	—	—
Alumni records	5	4	1	20
Residence halls	5	4	—	—
Other activities [c]	14	10	1	1

[a] Future Use category in this and succeeding tables represents predictions by computer directors of uses to which they intend to put computer equipment in the future.

[b] Percentages in column 4 represent the percentage increase over present use (column 1).

[c] This includes scholastic probation, research, mailings, sorority rush, job placement services, student elections, and evaluating service.

More institutions use their computers for registration work than for any other single purpose, as is shown in Table 2–3. In most cases the computer is used simply as a machine to record returns from the advisors and sectioners who work their way through the familiar long lines of students in the campus gymnasium. But in a few institutions, notably Purdue and the University of Massachusetts, with many more to follow, computers have been programed to work out the details of the student's class schedule and to match the schedule to sections and classrooms. At Purdue, for example, students select their desired courses in conference with their faculty counselors. Then the computer, an IBM 7090, begins the task of sectioning, making sure that the student has time out for lunch, employment, or other necessary activities. If a particular section is full, the computer rather than a human sectioner revises the student's schedule to place him in another section of the same course. Occasionally the computer cannot work out a compatible schedule for the student and rejects his selection of courses, but the rejection rate is usually only 6 per cent of the total. The computer also handles the inevitable drops and adds which occur after the initial phase of registration. In addition to using the computer for the design of the individual student's course schedule, Purdue administrators are also programing a computer to produce a master schedule of courses each semester. This master schedule takes into account a great variety of factors such as available physical space, faculty requirements, and anticipated student enrollments.[8]

In the area of student affairs the use of computers for registration was followed closely by their use for grade recording and other bookkeeping on the student. Grade records can subsequently be used for automatic print-outs of honors or failing lists and the analysis of student degree requirements by the computer. At the University of Washington the computer works out the grade average for each student. For those who fall below a specified average the computer then addresses a printed letter of expulsion. The student has an opportunity to appeal his expulsion to his dean if he chooses, but the dismissal is initially carried out by the computer. At the University of Illinois and several other institutions the computer is also used to analyze the grading patterns of faculty members, a development which causes no small amount of uneasiness in the academic community.

A majority of the institutions in our survey have also employed the services of computers in handling the admission of students. As in the case of student registration the computer frequently does little more than sort out the information contained on the student applications. But in an increasing number of institutions computers are used to evaluate and, in effect, to "decide" on the admissibility of the bulk of student applicants. Essentially the computer is instructed to calculate weighted high-school grade averages, test scores, and other measurable factors specified by the administrator and to provide lists of those students who are clearly admissible, clearly inadmissible, or marginal. The admissions officer then concentrates his attention on the marginal cases, hopefully weighing more subjective factors than those programed in the computer.

A number of other student activities have also drawn the attention of

[8] See James F. Blakesley, *Computer Scheduling at Purdue University* (Lafayette, Ind., mimeo., 1963) and *Computer Drop and Add Operations* (Lafayette, Ind., mimeo., 1964). For a description of procedures at the University of Massachusetts, See H. Hills Skillings, *Computer Class Scheduling: Experience at the University of Massachusetts* (Amherst: Office of Institutional Studies, University of Massachusetts, 1962).

the computer. Student tests are sometimes scored and analyzed by computers. Five institutions in our survey use computers for records and assignments in student residence halls. Two institutions use computers in their student job placement services, and two have even turned to computers to solve that most delicate of problems, the compilation of bids and choices for sorority rush.

As computers are used to handle more and more of the workload in the administration of student affairs, university officials have become edgy about contentions that they are creating a mechanistic system which ignores the student as a person. "The only time this school treated me like an individual," lamented one student to a college president, "was when I bent my IBM card." One admissions officer reported to us that "ninety percent of our applications are untouched by human hands." A fourth of the administrators in our survey said that they had encountered charges of dehumanization as a result of the use of computers. Most of these charges appear to come from the students themselves, although faculty members are another common source of complaint.

With virtual unanimity the college officials surveyed in this report denied, however, that university administration was becoming more impersonal under the impact of automation. Or, as one university official told us, "data processing computers may 'dehumanize' but without them we're inhumane." Registrars and admissions officers, for example, commonly argue that use of the computer makes it possible to deal with the student on a personal basis by freeing administrators from the burden of clerical work that would otherwise consume an increasing proportion of their time in face of expanding enrollments and the increased range and complexity of university course offerings. From this perspective the computer is looked upon as a device which takes over the day-to-day chores of administration, while the college official is left free to conduct interviews in depth with students and to give close personal attention to their problems.

It can also be contended, although admissions officers did not usually argue this way, that the computer itself has certain characteristics such as speed and versatility in operation that enable it in certain areas to give each student a degree of personal concern that no system of human administration would today find workable on a large campus. It is conceivable, for example, that criteria for the appraisal and selection of entering students can be much more complex and sophisticated when these processes are administered by a high-speed piece of electronic equipment than when they must be devised and applied by overworked admissions officers. And in scheduling classes a computer may be instructed to try an almost unlimited number of combinations before it rejects a proposed schedule. At the present time the computer may actually work through an average of thirty or more combinations for each student in normal registration procedure. It is questionable whether a human scheduler would have the time or patience to approximate this effort. Carried to its logical extreme this argument would suggest that the student is more likely to have his individual and perhaps idiosyncratic characteristics taken into account when he confronts banks of computers than when he deals with rows of clerks.

Nevertheless, college officials are wary of the possibility that the use of computers will give their institution a reputation for "impersonality" which will deter highly qualified students from applying for admission. At two of the institutions visited in this survey, where the use of computers in the selection of students is quite advanced, strenuous efforts have been made to publicize the fact that personal attention is still being given to each individual application. As one registration official put it in explaining his institution's use of automation in the admissions process, "Electronic data processing equipment and methods have not depersonalized the admissions process. They have simplified the handling of this great volume of material and increased the time admissions personnel can devote to the careful and equitable *evaluation* and *review* of records. Time saved in information retrieval and preliminary recording can now be devoted to personal interviews, clarifying problem situations and developing more realistic deadlines. In this process the 'numbering' of a candidate has been unavoidable and beneficial."[9] So far, at least, it thus appears to be highly important to some universities to avoid the public image of being unduly automated or inhumanly efficient.

This is not, of course, universally true. Miles and Hartford report the case of one institution where "the computer was being used to produce the President's letter of appointment to the academic staff."[10] While such a procedure may not in fact be any more impersonal than a form letter typed out by a secretary, it is hard to conceive of a method of operation more likely to convey an image of soulless administration to the faculty. But in the case of the student at a highly automated university, it is likely to be the rule rather than the exception that any letters he receives from the administration will be turned out by machines.

As a matter of fact, in spite of the assertions by administrators that computers create potentially more personal relationships with students, and notwithstanding the genuine efforts made at many institutions to

[9] William Starkweather, *Electronic Data Processing of Admissions: Handling of Student Applicants at the University of Massachusetts* (Amherst: Office of Institutional Studies, University of Massachusetts, 1963), p. 5.

[10] Miles and Hartford, *A Study of Administrative Uses of Computers*, pp. 8–9.

preserve a spirit of individual attention, the movement in university administration appears to be more in the direction of impersonal automation than away from it. In student admissions, for example, the idea of allowing computers to make the decisions on the clear-cut cases is quite defensible from an administrative point of view. Statistically, personal evaluations produce almost the same results as the computer evaluations as long as the criteria are the same. But one main characteristic of the computer is that it requires quantifiable standards of measurement such as grade averages and test scores. There is an overpowering pressure at most institutions we visited to make those quantifiable standards the critical standards for admission. Personality and motivation, then, are likely to be influential factors only for the students who are classified in a marginal group, while the destiny of the others is decided on the basis of quantified standards alone. And while admissions officers and others who use quantification can present strong evidence to support the accuracy of their predictions about student performance, their evidence may do little to create favorable attitudes among the students who are subjected to computer analysis and decision.

Financial Affairs

The use of computers for financial administration has proved to be somewhat less controversial than their use in student affairs. An example of a well-developed computer system for financial analysis is the University of California's central Data Processing Service, with units in both southern and northern California, which handles routine financial accounting for the entire university system. It performs all general accounting, including accounts payable, general ledger accounting, fiscal closing, and payroll. Converting the routine data to management information, the California computers produce budget reports and analyses, overhead cost studies, and monthly and quarterly reports of payroll statistics. And now that the University of California has acquired a workable backlog of data on magnetic tape, it is planning to use this data to construct a model of the university which will provide budgetary projections over the next decade. For the most part, however, financial administrators in state institutions use their computers in the tedious work of payroll and general accounting. Less than half of the institutions in our survey use computers for general inventories or budget preparation, and only a fourth use computers for cost analysis (see Table 2–4).

Physical Plant Management

The management of space has proved to be particularly amenable to computer applications, for the physical space of the campus is relatively easy to quantify and to record. Thus, as shown in Table 2–5, about a third of the colleges and universities responding to our questionnaire have used computers to record complete inventories of the space available in all buildings on their campuses. Once the basic inventory is available, officials responsible for the physical plant may use the data as the basis for assigning classroom and office space. Computers can also give the space administrator intricate data on the costs of constructing and maintaining buildings and rooms. Much of the information on the physical plant could be obtained without computers, but the speed and variety with which computers can display such information have made them especially valuable to administrators.

TABLE 2–4: USE OF COMPUTERS BY STATE COLLEGES AND UNIVERSITIES IN FINANCIAL ADMINISTRATION

	Present Use		Future Use	
Activity	No. of Schools (1)	% of Total (n = 134) (2)	No. of Schools (3)	% Increase[a] (4)
General accounting	100	75	19	19
Payroll	100	75	15	15
General inventories	59	44	25	43
Budget preparation	53	40	32	60
Cost analysis of operations	36	27	24	67
Investment records and analysis	13	10	12	92

[a] Percentages in column 4 represent the percentage increase over present use (column 1).

TABLE 2–5: USE OF COMPUTERS BY STATE COLLEGES AND UNIVERSITIES IN PHYSICAL PLANT MANAGEMENT

	Present Use		Future Use	
Activity	No. of Schools (1)	% of Total (n = 134) (2)	No. of Schools (3)	% increase[a] (4)
Space inventories	54	40	37	69
Space cost analysis	16	12	32	200
Assignment of classroom space	14	10	46	328
Assignment of office space	6	4	18	300

[a] Percentages in column 4 represent the percentage increase over present use (column 1).

The Central Office on the Use of Space at the University of Illinois has employed computers to compile a complete picture of instructional space available at each hour of the day for the entire university. The office has also developed detailed figures on the usage of all campus space—whether it is employed for research, teaching, extension, or administrative activity. These figures are stored on tape and can be recalled by the computer on command in almost any combination desired.

Policy Planning

Once a university builds up a sufficient backlog of information about its physical plant, students, faculty, and pattern of financial activities, it can contemplate the more ambitious effort of general policy planning and analysis on computers, which encompasses such activities as institutional research and long-range campus planning. It is in these areas that there is a compelling need for instruments which can integrate and correlate highly complex data, a job that is the stock in trade of the electronic computer.

Using computers, a director of institutional research is able to work out enrollment projections with elaborate detail. Computers can furnish prompt answers to such questions as the following. How many students from a given county will be enrolled in the university by 1968 if admissions standards remain the same, or, alternatively, if they are raised to a specified new level? What is the socio-economic background of the student body? How many square feet of new classroom space will be needed if the enrollment is increased by five thousand students? Computers can also analyze population trends to predict demographic changes in the student body. They can provide budgetary estimates and perform cost studies

TABLE 2–6: USE OF COMPUTERS BY STATE COLLEGES AND UNIVERSITIES FOR POLICY PLANNING

Activity	Present Use		Future Use	
	No. of Schools (1)	% of Total (n = 134) (2)	No. of Schools (3)	% Increase[a] (4)
Long-range planning	13	10	23	176
Institutional research	69	51	30	44
Simulation of institutional operations	6	4	17	283

[a] Percentages in column 4 represent the percentage increase over present use (column 1).

which reach beyond the practical capacity of human operators. Such computer applications are underway in over half of the institutions using computers in our survey (see Table 2–6).

The data developed in the purely routine work of computers is thus being recast increasingly into reports and studies that aid administrative officers in their policy decisions. The accumulation of such management information, as indicated in Table 2–7, appears to be a significant halfway point between the strictly routine and the most advanced forms of computer uses. At the University of Massachusetts, for example, programed processing of student admissions applications paved the way for "a weekly program which summarizes the most relevant data on each applicant and arranges this in tabular form, giving the relative weights assigned each factor. Thus a ready comparison and the relative standing of each candidate is known at a glance. . . . Also, a weekly statistical tabulation of applications is made. These lists subsequently become useful for analyzing demand trends, levels of admission standards, and as base data for studies on multiple applications."[11]

The availability of fresh management information has been a blessing to most university administrators, who reported to us that they felt much more confident about their decisions when they were backed by solid and systematic information drawn from the computers. The only recurrent complaint about computer reports was that they were sometimes prepared simply because the computer was able to perform the feat and not because the administrator really needed the information. As a result, a computer office that floods an administrator with information may be disappointed to learn that its reports end up in a wastebasket rather than on the desk of the president.

Few universities have ventured above the level of management information in their administrative computer uses, even though the research computers used by the faculty may be involved in high-level problem analysis. Up to the present time university administrators have been most interested in finding faster or cheaper ways to carry out their present responsibilities, not in administrative experimentation. What administrators have wanted most are devices to break the log jams of routine work piling up in their offices. To the extent that computers have promised to break those log jams, the administrators have been highly receptive to their use. For most of these routine jobs computers can be relatively limited in their problem-solving ability. In recent years computer companies have developed relatively inexpensive computers which can process huge volumes of informa-

[11] Leo F. Redfern, "The Calculating Administrators: Experience with Electronic Computers at the University of Massachusetts," *State Government*, Vol. 36 (Summer, 1963), p. 186.

TABLE 2–7: SUMMARY: COMPUTERS AND UNIVERSITY ADMINISTRATION

Level of Sophistication	Financial Administration	Physical Plant Management	Student Affairs	Policy Planning
Routine, programed procedures (most administrative uses are concentrated at this level)	Accounting Payroll Inventories Budget preparation Investment records	Space inventories Assignment of classrooms and offices	Processing admissions applications Grade records Registration processing Testing Student services General student records	Personnel records Alumni records Population data
Management information (a growing area of application, based upon data derived from routine procedures)	Instructional cost studies Investment portfolio analysis Comparative budget analysis	Studies of building and maintenance costs Classroom and office utilization studies Traffic pattern analysis	Admissions data Teaching load, course loads, etc., of faculty Analysis of dropouts and retentions Grading patterns in departments	Faculty and nonacademic personnel retention and replacement studies Analysis of alumni distribution and support
Advanced programed analysis and nonprogramed decision making (still largely unexploited except in a few universities)	Cost-benefit analysis of budgetary alternatives to determine optimum choice On-line computer monitoring of all business transactions Prediction of investment opportunities	Actual design of optimum building arrangements Space cost-benefit analysis, with computer solutions to best choices	Simulation of student enrollment patterns in the future under varying conditions Analysis of student creativity and predicted performance to determine admissions	Complete models of the institution for use in long-range planning Computer appraisal of faculty and nonacademic job applicants

tion. The IBM 1401 and 1620, for example, are capable of carrying on many of the administrative chores of a university such as payroll processing, student grade recording, and maintaining an inventory of campus space. They have been snapped up by large and medium-size universities, and even many small institutions have found it economically feasible to install the new computers.

By contrast, only a small number of institutions have made use of their great research computers for administrative work. These research computers are designed primarily to solve complicated problems requiring long computation times. They are not as well adapted to turning out large volumes of simple data at low cost. It is reasonable to assume that as college administrators acquire sophistication in the problem-solving capacities of research computers, they will turn increasingly to these computers for administrative purposes.

This administrative use of research computers by educational institutions will be facilitated by recent changes in manufacturers' policies governing the acquisition of computers. The principal manufacturer of electronic data-processing equipment in this country, International Business Machines, has commanded a massive share of the computer market for many years. (Today well over 90 per cent of the computers in universities are IBM.) Traditionally the company has offered low rental and purchase prices to educational institutions for computers used exclusively for research and instructional purposes. A university might receive as much as a 60 per cent allowance in purchasing computers as long as it did not use this equipment for administrative or commercial purposes. Regular administrative computers, on the other hand, were sold with only a 20 per cent allowance. Not so long ago, however, IBM made some changes in its allowance policy and specified that no new computers would be sold at the 60 per cent allowance rate. At the same time it lifted some of its restrictions on the use of the newly purchased computers, permitting them to be employed for administration as well as research. Although it is too soon to assess the effects of such policy changes, it is possible that more research computers will be used in the future for administrative work. Since research computers have a capacity for very high-level problem analysis, this may also mean that universities will be inclined in the future to try out more advanced types of administrative problem solving on computers.

Perhaps of more importance in the long run, new generations of computers designed for the late 1960's and 1970's will have the capacity to perform analytical work and routine information processsing with comparable efficiency, thus blurring the distinction that has existed in the present crop of computers. Therefore, both in terms of changing designs and in terms of the ideas which guide the use of computers, the years ahead portend significant changes for university administration.

THE BRAVE NEW WORLD OF COMPUTERS

The future of computer applications has often been highly exaggerated and misunderstood. Newspaper cartoonists delight in portraying the giant computer that outsmarts its human operator. And the bulletin boards of university computer centers are usually well stocked with the current jokes about the robot invasion. When all the dire warnings about *1984* have been cast aside, however, the plans of computer practitioners are impressive enough in their own right.

The construction of a statistical model of an entire university on a computer is no longer a distant vision. Several universities, including the University of Maryland, Purdue University, and the University of California, are already actively engaged in the groundwork for developing such models of their institutions. Most of these models are simply symbolic representations of the elements of the university which the program planner chooses to feed into the computer. A model may be as restricted or as complete as the model builder chooses. A limited model can be constructed purely for the purpose of analyzing the problems of dormitory space, without regard to budgets, classrooms, or faculty. But the possibility of constructing fully comprehensive models holds out great attraction for some venturesome administrators. A model might include real or hypothetical data about student bodies, faculties, budgets, library books, buildings, levels and varieties of courses, and almost any other quantifiable data that could be included on a computer program. The analyst could then simulate the effects of changing any of the variables upon the total system. For example, it is possible to simulate the probable effects of an increase in the number of graduate students on the budget, the faculty, the physical plant, and the library. While the accuracy of the simulation is only as sound as the data, the extensive backlog of information now available to model builders furnishes a comprehensive basis for analysis based on simulations.

One variation of computer simulation is an academic planning "game" developed at New Mexico State University.[12] Although the "game" may be played without a computer, it is adapted to more extensive applications when used with one. Essentially the game is designed to permit academic administrators to work through problems with hypothetical but fairly

[12] See John Forbes, *The College and University Planning Game* (University Park: New Mexico State University Planning Tool Center, 1963). Forbes was then the Director of Institutional Studies and Development at the university.

realistic data in order to gain experience for the decisions they will make in actual administration. The game encourages players to think in terms of the relationships of a number of factors and to become aware of the effects a single decision will have upon all areas of the simulated university. A complex scoring arrangement gives the players a means of evaluating the quality of their judgments. The university game thus borrows from techniques which have been in use for some time in military and industrial circles, where games have been used for the training of decision makers and for the analysis of alternative policies.[13]

Another future use of the computer lies in the area of heuristic problem solving in novel, unprogramed situations. This concept of "nonprogramed" decisions has been given prominence in the work of Herbert Simon, among others. Simon distinguishes between routine, repetitive data-processing procedures which can be written for the computer as a formal program or set of instructions—these he identifies as "programed decisions"—and novel, unstructured, exploratory analyses, which he labels "nonprogramed decisions." Some advanced computers can now be given a set of rough instructions instead of highly detailed programs and can proceed to attack a unique problem even though it may be poorly defined. In a sense, these "nonprogramed" activities of computers are somewhat analogous to the trial-and-error method that appears to characterize human thinking. The computer is instructed to solve part of a problem at a time, working by rough increments toward a general solution. Simon and Allen Newell, have developed a "General Problem Solver" program for a computer which is based on step-by-step analysis rather than on a completely comprehensive analysis of facts within the computer memory. So far, however, most of the work in heuristic problem solving is still in the experimental stage.[14] No university has reached this level of administrative analysis, although a number of officials are intensely interested in its possibilities.

While these experimental techniques will surely have their day in the practical world of university administration, it is likely that they will be preceded by still another modern application of the computer which is occupying the talents of many computer experts—the development of a total administrative information system built around the electronic computer.[15] In the complete information system all relevant historical institu-

[13] See, for example, R. P. Bennet *et al.*, *SIMPAC Users' Manual* (Santa Monica, Calif.: System Development Corporation, 1962), which is a handbook for model construction on digital computers. The term SIMPAC stands for "simulation package."

[14] Simon, *The New Science of Management Decision*, pp. 14–34.

[15] For a clear discussion of such a proposed system by one of the pioneers in the development of total information systems for universities, see John W. Hamblen, *Total Information Systems Design for a University* (a paper prepared for a workshop of System Development Corporation, Santa Monica, Calif., May 9, 1963, mimeo.).

tional data is fed into a computer system to be stored and placed on call for university officials. Current information such as enrollment figures, classroom use, running budget totals, personnel data, and other items can be placed in the computer on a continuing basis. Some universities have made plans to feed their information to the computer by means of teleprocessing units so that virtually instantaneous status reports are available to administrators. Under a fully operational management information system a university president could monitor the administrative operation of his institution in the same way in which a modern general, using computerized communication networks, can observe the progress of a military action. While the university president might read his information instead of viewing it on a giant battle screen, the basic method for bringing the information to him would be similar to the techniques that aid the military commander.

Computer manufacturers have been particularly interested in the concept of total information systems. Once a university accepts the principle of integrated data processing, the need for computer equipment is inescapable. For this reason several computer companies have directed their attention to the development of information-processing plans built around their own brand of computer hardware. The company is then in a position to offer a package deal to a college or university—a systematic plan of management, a kit of computer programs designed to handle specific administrative routines, the computer and its accessories, a computer language, and even a training program for computer operators.

Within university administrations, support for a total information system comes from a variety of sources. Some presidents have been particularly interested in the managerial possibilities of a fully integrated data-processing plan. Directors of institutional research have been quick to recognize the possibilities in such a plan for their research needs. In other cases, faculty mathematicians or physical scientists have worked with computers in their own research and have visualized the administrative implications of a total approach to management information. In the final analysis, the new concept of a completely integrated information system may prove to be the most significant element in the computer revolution in higher education, for it has the capacity to affect not only the routine management procedures of a university, but its administrative structure as well.

COMPUTERS AND ADMINISTRATIVE STRUCTURE

Since the total information system is still a plan and not a reality in American colleges and universities, any judgments about the influence that such a system will ultimately have on organizational structure must be highly tentative. But the computer systems already in existence, even though they are not total in their design, furnish some evidence of the effects of computers on the way that educational institutions organize their affairs.

Initially, the university administrator is faced with the elementary problem of placing the computer hardware and personnel into the administrative hierarchy. In 91 per cent of the state colleges and universities sampled in our survey the computers have been installed in a central computer facility, which is responsible directly to a high administrative official, usually a vice-president. Some institutions created the central computer service at the same time that computers were acquired, but in several cases the university gave jurisdiction over computers to some pre-existing administrative agency. At the University of Illinois, for example, a Statistical Service Unit had been in operation since 1948, working with machine calculators designed to serve a variety of university offices. When IBM 1401 computers were installed in 1961 the university placed them in this central unit and substantially expanded the responsibilities of the office. By early 1963 the unit added a second 1401 computer and both were placed on multiple-shift operation. In three years the work of the Statistical Service Unit increased roughly 1,000 per cent. The staff tripled and in 1964 the office added a third computer system to handle its growing workload.

Only 9 per cent of the state institutions in our sample have allowed individual university offices to acquire their own administrative computers and to use them more or less exclusively for their own work. At the University of Wisconsin, for example, one computer system is used by the registrar, while another is used for general administrative purposes, and a third system is used for hospital administration. At the University of Minnesota a few computers were placed in administrative offices but many administrative routines were still carried on by hand or machine methods.

The economic incentive to centralize computers is a compelling one. Except in the largest universities, it is doubtful if a single administrative office can generate enough work to keep a medium-size computer fully employed. And since computers may cost around a quarter of a million dollars or rent for several thousand dollars a month, the university can scarcely afford to let such an expensive piece of equipment lie idle for many hours of the day. Moreover, computer systems require highly trained programers and operators and it is often not practical to hire them on a part-time basis. In view of the costs of both hardware and personnel, the most common choice has been to establish a fully centralized computer office.

Once a central computer facility becomes a going concern, still other changes are likely to be in the offing. Computer programs require standardized information in uniform language, and this often means that university offices will have to recast many of their reporting and accounting procedures in order to make their work compatible with the computer program. This standardization, in turn, sometimes requires new personnel and skills. Unlike some business firms, universities have not gone through a phase of technological unemployment as a result of using computers for administration. Because higher education has been a growth industry during the period since World War II, the increasing automation of the campus has not led to any reduction in the administrative work force, as contrasted with other areas of white-collar employment where the introduction of computers has brought about considerable unemployment.[16] But it is clear that there would have been a much more substantial increase in clerical personnel in higher education in the past decade if computers had not been introduced.

The emergence of the computer specialist has also been an important new factor in the administrative development of universities. Often the director of a centralized computer office is a highly trained statistician, quite frequently with a Ph.D. in mathematics, who speaks the language of both the professor and the administrator. Most of the computer directors interviewed in the course of this study were strong advocates of the uncompartmentalized systems approach to university administration. By virtue of their familiarity with administrative procedures, the computer directors are in a position to suggest a great variety of reforms which their offices are capable of undertaking. Consequently, officials responsible for admissions, registration, or budgeting, among other activities, often seek the advice of the computer director about ways to improve their own operations with the assistance of the central computer facility.

The computer director therefore often discusses admissions as part of a complete data-processing procedure involving registration, record keeping, advising, classroom scheduling, right down through graduation and alumni records. This tendency to cut through departmental boundaries is one of the chief characteristics of the systems approach to administration, for it is based on the perception of the university as an organic unity rather than as an administrative structure broken into distinct departments and

[16] See Ida R. Hoos, "When the Computer Takes Over the Office," *Harvard Business Review*, Vol. 38 (July–August, 1960), pp. 102–12. In a two-year study of nineteen firms in the San Francisco Bay area, the author found that computers were highly unsettling on clerical personnel. For a contrasting view, see Barton A. Fields, "Introducing Continuous Change in Pennsylvania," *Public Administration Review*, Vol. 22 (September, 1962), pp. 134–38. This article suggests that clerical personnel may in fact be retained for considerably more interesting jobs than they had before.

agencies. By contrast, some, though certainly not all, traditional administrators view their operations in terms of separate boxes on an organization chart.

Yet in no case did we observe that the systems approach had taken over completely from the old pattern of compartmentalized structures. Instead the systems approach, with its center of gravity in the computer facility of the university, is simply co-existing with the older organizational approach. Neither point of view has yet been triumphant. And one of the chief reasons why the transformation has not been more complete is that the issues involve considerably more than the boxes on the organization chart.

COMPUTERS AND ADMINISTRATIVE AUTHORITY

Although most of the emphasis in computer literature is on the contribution of this equipment to administrative efficiency, the introduction of computers and automatic data processing also exerts a less obvious influence on power, policy, and strategy in university operation. Computer experts argue correctly that there is no necessary connection between the centralization of information through computers and the centralization of administrative authority. Computing machines are quite indifferent to the distribution of power within a particular organization or the kind of values and preferences held by its personnel. This may be technically correct, but, in the institutions we have observed, there has been a definite centralization of authority corresponding to the centralization of information in a data-processing system.

In a recent study for the RAND Corporation, Edward F. R. Hearle and Raymond J. Mason advocate that units of state and local government establish a "Unified Information System" embracing all their administrative activities. This centralized information system, they argue, "provides only for the central storage and processing of data according to the instructions of participating agencies; it does not in any way prescribe how data are to be used, a matter for each agency to determine for itself."[17]

Hearle and Mason believe that the assets of a fully centralized system far outweigh any disadvantages. A common memory for different government agencies would eliminate, or certainly reduce, the duplication of effort by agencies which gather and use comparable information. Under a centralized system, a single input of data would serve all agencies equally well. The availability of data in a central place would also permit correlations and integrations that are quite impossible in a decentralized system of administration. Since computers operate at such great speed, the

[17] *A Data Processing System for State and Local Governments* (Englewood Cliffs, N.J.: Prentice-Hall, 1963), p. 57.

transactions between a central computer unit and an operating agency "can be essentially instantaneous, thus removing one of the major traditional objections to centralized information storage."[18] Even the problem of protecting the confidential nature of information in a central storage can be solved by installing a system of private keys to operate the remote control equipment. In this way it is possible that information can be kept more confidential under the unified arrangement than under the loosely controlled procedures which presently exist. The central information system Hearle and Mason envisage would thus eliminate duplication and make information infinitely more usable without at the same time slowing down the administrative process or violating the privacy of information.

In a university setting, however, the establishment of such a centralized information system raises sensitive issues. Strictly hierarchical organizations accept the idea that information processed by any constituent unit should be subject to surveillance by higher administrative echelons. In theory, at least, the subordinate is not expected to conceal anything from his superior. But in a university setting, where authority is not hierarchical and where individual departments operate with a great deal of autonomy, departmental officers may be understandably reluctant to supply information to the central authority when their position of independent power may largely depend on the fact that they alone have access to certain kinds of data.

In the area of space utilization, for example, many universities have long permitted individual departments or colleges to maintain virtual title to their classroom and office space. Very often in fact a chemistry department may be the only agency in the university that really knows how much space it has and how it is used. But with the advent of computer storage systems, universities can inventory every room in every building on the campus, keeping track of departmental occupancy, square feet of area, and general use of each room. More importantly, computers can display this information in a variety of comparative modes, so that a university administrator can tell at a moment's notice exactly how many square feet of office space the chemistry department occupies in comparison with the physics department.

Once the information is centralized in this manner the administration is at least the equal of the department in disputes over the use of physical space. In actual practice, however, the administration may quickly get the upper hand, for it is administrators who control the operation of the computer facility; the individual department does not. The computers are often located in or near the administration building, which may create a psycho-

[18] *Ibid.*, p. 57.

logical obstacle to their use by departments. Moreover, the administration is an habitual user of the computer, while departments often must seek special permission to use the computer facility. Thus, even if departments enjoy theoretically equal access to the computers and the information they contain, in reality they confront barriers to the use of computers which do not impede the administration.

One university official reported that some units in his institution were reluctant to permit the conversion of their records from punch cards to magnetic tape, partly because of "a disinclination to give up the power which comes with being sole 'custodian of the cards.' " In other words, magnetic tapes were centrally stored in the computer facility, while punch cards had been kept in files in the other offices of the university. The changeover to tapes left each university agency considerably more vulnerable to scrutiny than it had been in the past.

In many universities information that is processed and stored on administrative computers is not regarded as the common property of the entire university. Individual departments usually know their own computer-generated salary and space figures, but only the administration may know how these figures compare with other departments. At one institution in our survey individual departments were given comparative data on instructional load and grading practices only after code names had been substituted for other departments. In this way, as an administrator explained, the departments "can't start drawing all of the information together to start using against each other." Nor, it might be added, can the departments use this information as easily to question the decisions of the administration.

Such restriction of information by a university administration is a matter of policy and not a necessary outgrowth of the use of computers. But the presence of a centralized computer facility gives a logical underpinning to administrative monopoly of information. As noted earlier, computers are extremely expensive, and the economies to be gained from a central facility are substantial. Departments would have great difficulty in acquiring computers of their own which they could use to prepare competing data. Ordinarily the sheer complexity and expense of programing and processing administrative information is sufficient to prevent departments of the university from engaging in an extended duel with the administration.

The central computer facility itself is customarily looked upon as the completely neutral staff instrument of the administration or the entire university. Yet the extent to which the computer agency is in fact divorced from policy-making is heavily dependent upon the philosophy which governs the operation of the computer center and the top administrative personnel of the university. For example, one institutional research director complained that he was constantly hobbled in his efforts to analyze data because he was required to depend upon a separate computer facility for all programing and processing. The computer center, by its power to determine its own programing and operating schedule, could decide which agencies of the university would do their work quickly and which agencies would do their work slowly. In effect this power devolves upon the computer director, who is generally regarded as a servant of the administration.

In one multi-campus university, a conflict between the centralized data-processing system and a local campus registrar highlighted several of the issues that accompany the conversion to computers. From the beginning the registrar refused to go along with a plan to convert his registration system to computers unless he could control his own equipment. His opposition was not to computers as such, but to the principle of a centralized system. He contended that his manual methods were both more economical and faster than the work of the central computer facility. He pointed gleefully to the fact that campuses using the central computers for grade reporting were as much as two weeks behind the campus which did not depend upon the centralized system.

The computer director, on the other hand, argued that any delays in central computer operations were the product of transition and that a centralized procedure would prove to be faster in the long run. It took almost a year, however, for the central facility to streamline its operations sufficiently to catch up with the manual methods and eventually to surpass them. Even so, the local registrar managed to convince his superiors that he should have a computer of his own rather than submit to the indignity of scheduling his work in the central unit.

A few university officials voice skepticism about the objectivity or competence of the programers employed by a central computer facility. Such skeptics believe that a programer who is biased can manipulate his program planning in essentially undetected ways in order to produce the data he wants. For this reason some university officials, resigned to the fact that they cannot have their own computers, make a strenuous effort to hire their own computer programers to eliminate the effects of any bias in the central organization.

Even in universities in which there is little controversy over the role of a computer center, the latent issues of authority and power lie close at hand. At one western university, for example, the registrar stoutly resisted proposals to convert his old-fashioned registration procedure to an automated system. Outwardly the question was simply one of administrative efficiency: would the new arrangement register students more quickly and more cheaply? Beneath the surface, however, lay another issue. The old system permitted departments to exercise a high degree of unilateral control over the admission of any student to their courses. The centralized computer registration system on the other hand required the departments to operate with uniform, programed criteria in admitting or rejecting students in their courses, since the computer could not take into account such intangibles as faculty judgments of students wanting to take particular courses. Several departments, sensing this potential loss of discretion, aligned themselves with the registrar in his oposition to change, not because of antagonism to efficiency but because they wanted to preserve their traditional autonomy. The real and largely obscured issue was not whether the new system would work faster and more accurately—there was strong evidence that it would— but whether it would take power away from some people and give it to others. With such conflicting interests at stake, the dispute could not readily be resolved in terms of narrow managerial considerations alone.

In point of fact, the good reasons which administrators give for converting to computers are not necessarily the real reasons. University presidents face formidable difficulties in effecting change within the highly diffuse structure of an academic institution. Faculty groups, research units, and even administrative offices often possess a degree of independence which permits them to resist or ignore instructions from the central administration. Given this condition of academic life, a university executive must sometimes resort to subtle strategies in bringing about change. A president may feel that the departments have acquired too much discretion over the admission of students to their courses, but he would find it difficult to make an outright declaration of policy to the effect that departments can no longer veto a student who has taken the formal prerequisites for a course he seeks to enter. Instead he may use the computer to centralize the power of decision over course admissions on the quite proper grounds that the computer system will not work unless uniform standards are employed. In this respect, therefore, the introduction of computers "very often permits other procedural and organizational changes because these are believed to be part of the computer 'package.' The computer, in effect, becomes the vehicle for other desired changes."[19]

Finally, beyond considerations of efficiency and internal control, the computer plays an important role as a showpiece to impress the outside world with the modernity of university administration. As the struggle for legislative appropriations grows intense state universities must draw upon

[19] Thomas L. Whisler and George P. Shultz, "Information Technology and Management Organization," in Shultz and Whisler (eds.), *Management Organization and the Computer* (New York: The Free Press of Glencoe, 1960), p. 21. The quotation is in reference to businesses, but the point is also relevant to universities.

any and all available strategies to ensure financial survival. One such strategy is to give the public and the state legislature every possible reason to believe that the university is being operated with maximum efficiency. And since computers have become key symbols of scientific management in business and industry, the incentive to install computers in public colleges and universities is intensified by the hope that the equipment will radiate an aura of efficiency about an institution's operations to the community at large.

One director of a machine calculating center at a state university told us that he was actually content with the older machine equipment but that he was adding a computer in the next biennium because he felt that the administration wanted the office to be more modern and because he would personally feel "unstylish" if he did not go along with the current fashion of using computers in university administration. But even if computers are introduced for motives of this kind, their technical capacities cannot be denied, and these capacities will eventually enable computers to bring about substantial changes in administrative structure and operation at any campus on which they are installed.[20]

One other important development which the advent of computers has greatly facilitated is the establishment of offices of institutional research —an aspect of the new science of management to be discussed in the chapter that follows. As a matter of fact the study of computers in higher education which Miles and Hartford conducted in 1962 showed that the administrative activity for which the highest percentage of institutions were using computers was institutional research.[21] The operations of a bureau of institutional research may thus be assisted, and in some cases expanded, by the accessibility of computers. Indeed, the development and exploitation of the analytical possibilities of the computer may actually point the way toward the establishment of a bureau of institutional research, as occurred at MIT.

To be sure, institutional research is not absolutely dependent upon the availability of automatic data-processing equipment. There has been a lively amount of institutional research on college campuses, particularly

[20] In a letter to the authors, one specialist on computer technology commented as follows with respect to the attitude of university administrators toward computers: "It has been said (I don't know who said it first) that university administrators go through three stages with respect to the use of computers for their needs. They are 1) absolutely against it at first, then accept it with 2) passive indifference, and finally make 3) unreasonable demands for services."

[21] *A Study of Administrative Uses of Computers*, pp. 6–7. However, a veteran institutional research director complained to us that "most institutional research offices have the very devil of a time getting to use the machines at all, and must accept a low priority for the use of odds and ends of machine time when the so-called bread and butter operations permit."

at the smaller private institutions, even without the benefit of computers or other automated aids to management analysis. Bennington College, for example, for a long time conducted a very careful program of appraising faculty members by sending questionnaires to students and alumnae—a type of research it is difficult to conceive of the larger institutions undertaking, with or without the use of computers.

Chapter Three

THE GROWTH OF INSTITUTIONAL RESEARCH

Institutional research lies at the heart of the trend toward the use of modern management techniques in higher education. While the nature and scope of this kind of activity has tended to elude precise definition in the past, it can be said that institutional research is a variegated form of organizational self-study designed to help colleges and universities gather an expanding range of information about their own internal operations and the effectiveness with which they are using their resources. By collecting such data, institutions hope to make informed judgments instead of guessing or relying on the intuitions of the administrator in framing decisions on university policy.

The kind of decisions affected by institutional research varies from one campus to another, depending on whether investigations are centered on students, faculty, cost of operations, or physical facilities. But an enterprising bureau of institutional research may probe into many dusty corners of university life, revealing, for example, that there is a much heavier workload in some departments than in others, that a high drop-out rate is present among the most promising students, or that the level of faculty salaries is putting a university at a serious competitive disadvantage in attracting talented scholars to its campus.

Sometimes the information gathered may simply bring alterations in administrative routine. On other occasions, however, it may trigger sharp disputes among departments, or a searching re-examination by top-level administrators of a university's goals and achievements. The establishment of an office of institutional research may also signal an important shift of power within the university hierarchy, since the data gathered through such an office may furnish a potent instrument of administrative planning and control.

Equally significant is the effect institutional research may have in reshaping the pattern of relations between a public institution of higher education and its external environment. The data made available by an IR office may be of considerable value to a public institution of higher education in refuting charges from state fiscal agencies and taxpayer groups that it is wasteful and inefficient in its use of appropriated funds. Or it may be highly useful in justifying requests for increased financial support. In this respect the growth of institutional research has served to strengthen state colleges and universities in their constant effort since World War II to obtain adequate financial support from the legislature.

By the same token, however, the development of institutional research as a tool of academic management is not without its perils for a state university. There is no way to guarantee that the data gathered will not ultimately be used against an organization as well as in its behalf, to detract from, rather than to enhance, its reputation for efficient management. One IR director somewhat ruefully described the techniques he was developing as "burglar's tools" which might eventually allow outsiders to gain entry into aspects of university decision from which they had previously been barred by the absence of reliable information. Even in the face of this danger, universities have been forced into institutional research by the recognition that they must gather accurate data about their own operations in self defense. Otherwise they may find themselves at the mercy of state officials with power to make decisions affecting the university on appropriations and other matters who will act on the basis of their own data, or on the basis of no information at all.

THE ORIGINS OF INSTITUTIONAL RESEARCH

It is only in the past few years that most colleges and universities have established offices or bureaus of institutional research. Prior to 1955 there were only 10 institutions of higher education in this country which could boast such offices. But by 1964 no less than 115 institutions reported having a bureau or official charged with responsibility for conducting institutional research. Figure 3–1 demonstrates this dramatic expansion during the past decade. Over 90 per cent of all the IR offices responding to our questionnaire were established between 1955 and 1964. The indications are that this trend will continue as pressures for the application of modern techniques of management to higher education mount in scope and intensity.

The growing interest in institutional research is also reflected by attendance at meetings and conferences dealing with this topic. In 1957, when the American Council on Education sponsored a nationwide conference on the subject of institutional self-study, it was hard put at first to locate individuals to whom invitations should be extended. Five years later there were over 60 people present at a national conference of institutional

FIGURE 3–1: THE EXPLOSION OF INSTITUTIONAL RESEARCH 1955–1964[a]

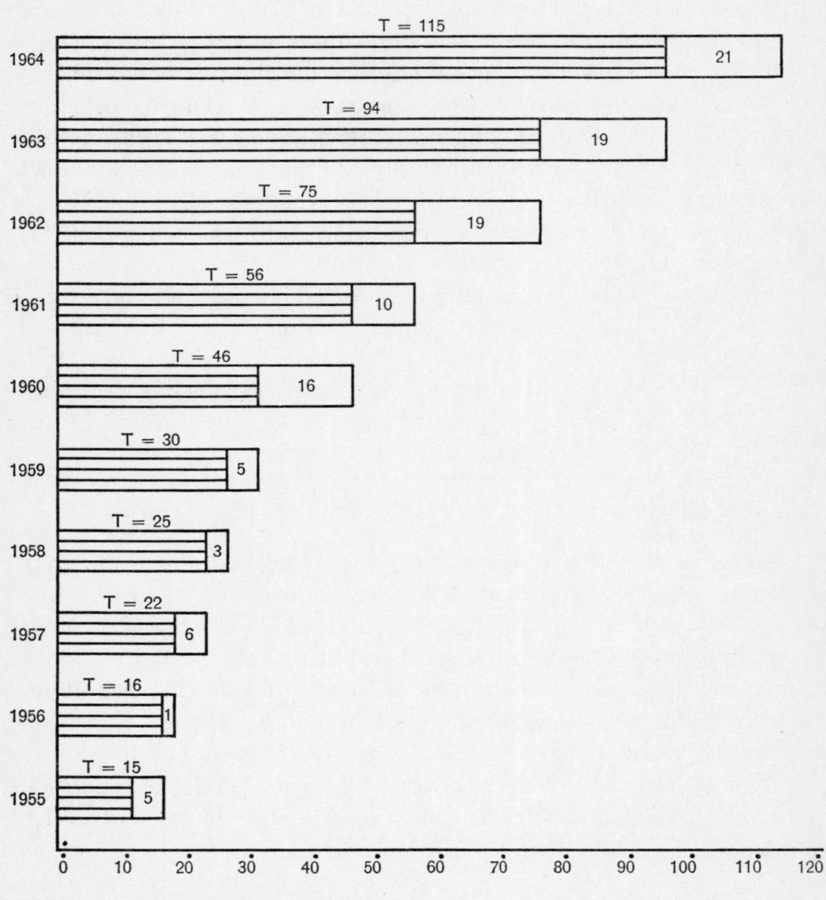

☐ New offices established during the year.
T = Cumulative total of IR offices in existence by end of year.
[a] Based on returns to IR questionnaire, Appendix B.

research officials held at Northern Illinois University,[1] and in 1963 over 200 attended a similar meeting at Wayne State University in Detroit.[2]

In part, these swelling figures reflect not so much an increase in the actual number of individuals engaged in institutional research as they do the growing tendency of those involved in such activity to identify themselves with this new role in academic administration. For a long time institutional research was carried on at a number of institutions in at least an embryonic way as a by-product of regular budgetary preparation, or in conjunction with studies of the university's building needs, or as a result of the persistent efforts of registrars and admissions officers to analyze the kind of student an institution was attracting and the quality of the record he was compiling after admission.

Institutional research was thus a standard procedure at a number of institutions of higher education in this country long before it made any appearance on their formal tables of organization. It is still performed in this informal way at many schools where it has not yet gained official recognition as a separate administrative function. In a survey published in 1961 of institutional research activity at schools having an enrollment in excess of 4,000, Howell and Carlson found that more than 80 per cent of the institutions responding employed staff members who were engaged in this activity on a part-time basis.[3]

Our own survey revealed that the size of an institution is a tremendously important factor in stimulating the development of institutional research. The larger an institution, the more likely it is to have established an IR office on campus. Of the schools in our study with an enrollment under 2,000 only a fraction more than 20 per cent indicated the presence of an office or person designated to carry on institutional research, as contrasted to more than 52 per cent of schools with enrollments between 2,000 and 10,000, and better than 72 per cent of those with a student population of 10,000 or above.[4]

INSTITUTIONAL RESEARCH IN OPERATION

Actually there has been widespread dispute in higher education as to what institutional research really is. In the past two principal schools of

[1] For the proceedings of this meeting see *Conference on Institutional Research in Higher Education*, Research Bulletin No. 6 (DeKalb, Ill.: Northern Illinois University, March 29–30, 1962).

[2] The proceedings of this meeting have also been published. See L. Joseph Lins (ed.), *The Role of Institutional Research in Planning* (Madison: Office of Institutional Studies, University of Wisconsin, 1963).

[3] Charles E. Howell and Milton E. Carlson, *Institutional Research* (DeKalb, Ill.: Northern Illinois University, 1961), p. 3.

[4] There is an association with region as well. See Appendix B, p. 149, for evidence regarding the high incidence of institutional research offices in the West.

thought on this subject have attracted considerable support. Some have felt that institutional analysis ought to deal primarily with administrative or housekeeping problems, space utilization and the like, thus remaining in effect a form of operations research as applied to the business aspects of campus management. Others have argued that it should not be confined to the "building and grounds" side of higher education but should go to the heart of the matter and appraise what is happening in the classroom. When the New England Board of Higher Education held a workshop on institutional research in 1962 it centered its attention on the administrative aspects of campus operations. There was sharp criticism of this approach as being too narrowly "bureaucratic" in its orientation, and in the following year the board conducted a workshop on institutional research which was devoted almost exclusively to questions of "academic effectiveness."[5]

The results of our own investigation provide evidence that the work of institutional research agencies today is primarily concerned with academic questions. Each agency was asked to describe its major work orientation by ranking several areas of university activity in order of their importance to the office. The major areas listed included students, faculty, finance, and physical planning. Out of the 124 schools responding to the question, 40 per cent listed students as being their first order of concern, while another 24 per cent indicated that faculty studies were of primary importance. If these two areas are grouped as research on questions of "academic effectiveness," then almost two-thirds of the responding agencies may be described as having primarily an academic orientation. On the other hand, 16 per cent of all schools listed finance as their major concern, while another 13 per cent ranked physical planning as the first order of importance. Some 29 per cent of all schools thus used institutional research chiefly for the study of housekeeping rather than academic problems.

The kind of activity in which any particular bureau of institutional research happens to engage is shaped by a variety of factors. In part it reflects the philosophy and interests of the individual in charge of the operation, particularly where the tasks of the IR office are loosely defined or where the research staff has some slack in its work schedule. One research director with a background in economics concentrates his research on cost studies and general financial problems. Another director with a particular interest in computers has devoted much of his time to the development of a comprehensive information system for his university

[5] See Raymond Castelpoggi (ed.), *Academic Effectiveness* (Amherst: University of Massachusetts, 1964).

based on the use of electronic data-processing equipment. Over a period of years a successful institutional research director thus has an opportunity to make the office a lengthened shadow of his own figure. This tendency for the interests of an institutional research director to shape the work of his office is heightened by the fact that most IR agencies employ only a limited number of professional personnel. More than 52 per cent of all the institutional research bureaus responding to our questionnaire employed but one professional staff employee, and 80 per cent of these agencies had no more than three professional staff members (see Appendix B, Table B–5).

External pressures also play an important role in determining the activity of an office of institutional study. Research must very often be directed at questions to which the outside community demands an answer, or that a university president feels will very shortly be asked. Much of the time of an office of institutional research may thus be consumed in dealing with emergencies which arise in an institution's relations with its environment. (And most public institutions have lived in a climate of crises, at least in the area of finance, since World War II.) For a considerable period of time after its establishment, the bureau of institutional research at the University of Massachusetts devoted a major portion of its energy to assisting in the university's efforts to free itself from a long-standing and confining range of restrictions by state agencies over its internal financial and personnel practices.

Because of the need to deal with trouble-shooting responsibilities of this kind, an office of institutional research ordinarily has very little opportunity to develop into an instrument of long-range planning, helping a university president to look ahead and anticipate the academic problems which his institution may confront in five or ten years. In this respect, of course, the plight of an IR office is not different from that of similar research units in other organizations, as, for example, the policy-planning staff in the State Department, which has tended over the years to be distracted from the task of diplomatic foresight by the need to confront crises in the everyday work of the department.

Some institutional research directors also take the view that too much of their time is taken up with repetitive projects of one kind or another—annual enrollment distributions, faculty workload studies, and the like. To avoid investing too much energy in this sort of recurring task, an IR director in the Midwest follows the practice of relinquishing jurisdiction over any study once it becomes clear that it will need to be undertaken on an annual or periodic basis. He feels that the chief threat to the effective functioning of an institutional research office is the possibility that it may become a purely fact-gathering agency, rather than participating in studies focused on fundamental policy decisions as they arise in the life of the university.

Many offices of institutional research do, however, engage in studies that are repetitive, and their image on the campus in some cases is that of agencies which carry on routine projects connected with the budget, enrollments, or some other recurring concern. This practice was defended by one IR director who pointed out that it is only through repeated studies of the same subject that important trends in academic life can be clearly identified—changes in the composition of the student body, for example. He also noted that many repetitive studies can be handled with the use of electronic data-processing equipment, and the time of professional employees in the institutional research office is not, therefore monopolized by such projects.

Considerations of diplomacy also have a distinct effect upon the work of an office of institutional research. At some institutions there has been a tendency for such offices to shy away from research concerned with areas that have traditionally lain within the jurisdiction of the faculty—curriculum, for example, or grading practices. Thus only a very low percentage of all IR bureaus listed curriculum analysis as their main order of business. For many faculty members the prospect of research by outsiders into the area of the classroom is, to adopt Herman Kahn's description of reactions to the possibility of nuclear war, a matter of "thinking about the unthinkable." At most of the institutions we visited institutional researchers carefully steered away from topics that might arouse such controversy.

At a few institutions, however, IR offices have attempted, with limited success, to give assistance to the faculty in studying matters at the core of the academic process. Institutional research at the University of Minnesota originated with the study of faculty problems—the recruitment and retention of academic staff, for example. The director of the agency has always worked closely with the faculty and seems generally to have been held in high esteem by university professors. It is only in recent years that the institutional research office at Minnesota has begun to lose its primary orientation toward the faculty. In response to requests from university officials for assistance in gathering data on costs and other management problems, an administrative research unit has been added to the Bureau of Institutional Research.

At the same time, however, the traditional role of the IR office in undertaking faculty-oriented studies continues to be carried on through its "general educational research unit." One of the principal functions of this division is to serve as a secretariat for faculty committees and to provide these committees with staff where necessary to carry out studies of academic programs. The bureau also provides a variety of services for individual faculty members. It will, for example, prepare and process teacher evaluation forms for any professor, upon his request and on a confidential basis, and it maintains a consulting service for faculty members who ask for help in making up examinations.

Efforts were made at Miami University in Ohio to give a similar focus to institutional research. To this end the Bureau of Institutional Research at the University was redesignated as an Instructional Research Service Unit. The director of this new agency sits with the faculty committee on Educational Policy and Planning to ensure a maximum of interaction between the agency and professors with an interest in university problems. Typical of its work, the Miami Instructional Research Service Unit conducted a study of whether an incoming freshman would be more or less likely to earn a high grade in a subject if he or she elected the university's honors program. With respect to the role of institutional research at Miami, a former president of the university commented, "We came to the conclusion at Miami that high-powered talent in the field of educational psychology and psychometrics should be devoted exclusively to instructional problems and not to the internal management problems of the university."

One of the most interesting applications of institutional research to instructional problems has occurred at the University of Washington. There an office with designated responsibility for "institutional educational research" undertook to experiment with student groupings in a new university dormitory to see whether the clustering of students by majors would increase the probability that they would successfully complete their academic careers. The experiment was part of a larger and more far-reaching effort to trace the relationship between student grouping and academic achievement. This kind of inquiry into space utilization is far more directly related to the teaching function than is usually the case with such studies.

The story did not have an altogether happy ending, however. When the students involved in the experiment discovered that they were, in effect, "being used as guinea pigs," a good many of them reacted very negatively to the whole affair. They particularly resented the fact that they had been subjected to study in this way without their own consent. After a heated debate over the project in the student newspaper and in dormitory councils, the university administration agreed to perform no further experiments without the consent of the participants. The concession was a victory for the protesting students, but it hobbled the researchers in their effort to establish control groups for their analysis.

At an institution like Minnesota, where the office of institutional research puts a good deal of emphasis upon problems that are requested by the academic staff, it has proven useful to co-opt the faculty into the institutional research operation by establishing a faculty advisory committee to oversee the research projects undertaken by the bureau. This has the result of legitimizing these studies in the eyes of many professors who might otherwise be hostile to institutional research. A faculty advisory committee can also play a useful role in helping an IR office avoid errors in research design which will invalidate the results of studies it may conduct. At two of the institutions visited there was faculty criticism of institutional research studies which overlooked significant factors involved in the problems under investigation. At one institution in the West, for example, the IR director had a reputation among faculty members for going off "half-cocked" with reports that were inadequate in conception or research technique.

However, even while research in this area has been subject to faculty criticism on the ground that the methods employed are far too unsophisticated, some university administrators have charged institutional research directors with being overly preoccupied with the niceties of methodology to the point where their studies lack application to practical university problems. Several of the university officials questioned in the course of this study complained that institutional research directors were far too much concerned with turning out reports that would bring them esteem in the eyes of their statistically oriented colleagues and not enough interested in undertaking studies that would contribute to the solution of actual problems with which the university was confronted. In short, IR directors may be caught between charges by one group than they are too professionally oriented in their research and complaints from another that they are not professional enough.

Since an institutional research office occupies a staff position on most campuses, its role in university operations is also shaped by the needs or inclinations of the official to whom it is responsible. Table 3–1 shows the

TABLE 3–1: CONTROL OF INSTITUTIONAL RESEARCH: OFFICIAL TO WHOM IR AGENCY REPORTS

University Official	% of Total (n = 120)
President	64
Vice-president	13
Dean of instruction	10
Executive dean	5
Provost	5
Other	3

pattern which emerged in this respect among the institutions responding to our questionnaire.

Obviously it is common practice for IR bureaus to report to the president of their institution, and presidents vary a good deal in the way in which they use these agencies. A university president may, for example, use such an office mainly for the purpose of answering the questionnaires with which most campuses are flooded. One IR official complained that his office was largely an administrative catch-all to handle minor problems delegated to it at the convenience of the president's office. Or a president may use institutional research to shore up his own administrative weaknesses. The head of one eastern university assigned his institutional research office the task of handling the development of physical facilities on the campus—largely, it was claimed, because of his own acute distaste for this aspect of his responsibilities.

This review of the various activities which institutional research offices undertake on university campuses might well suggest that there are as many different roles such offices can play as there are universities. Moreover, the definitions of institutional research to be found in the literature of higher education are similarly wide-ranging. As a matter of fact, if any single institutional research agency attempted to investigate all the areas assigned to it in some of these discussions, it would need a budget of astronomical size and a staff of extraordinary competence. Formal definitions of institutional research are breath-takingly eclectic, embracing virtually every problem institutions have faced since the rise of the medieval university.

Given the limitations of time and budgets under which they operate, however, individual offices of institutional research have often tended to specialize. Sometimes this means that the IR office becomes in effect the space utilization agency on campus, in the absence of any other agency which might assume this task. Moreover, a number of IR offices have taken on the planning function, with particular attention given to the development of physical facilities. As noted earlier, 13 per cent of all the offices of institutional research in our survey listed planning as their primary responsibility. At the University of Rhode Island the IR office devoted so much time to this planning role that the agency was eventually redesignated as the office of institutional research and planning. However, critics of the IR office at this university contended that institutional research tended to be submerged beneath the physical development function, to the point that the IR director spent most of his time deciding what kind of brick should be used in the construction of new buildings on the university campus.

PROBLEMS OF ORGANIZATION

The establishment of an institutional research agency within the organizational structure of a university may trigger sensitive reactions from other groups on campus. The fact that the faculty should look with suspicion upon the establishment of an office of institutional research in a university hierarchy is not surprising, in view of the common propensity of academic man to look with alarm upon any apparent extension in the power of university administration. What is not so generally recognized, however, is the extent to which the advent of such an office may arouse anxiety within the ranks of university administration itself.

A division of finance, for example, or a business manager's office, may well suspect that the new institutional research unit will pull some power out from under its own jurisdiction by conducting studies of fiscal administration. At two of the institutions visited there was evidence of considerable strain between institutional research and financial administrators growing precisely out of this kind of concern. While, from the remote perspective of the faculty member, university administration may appear monolithic, it is as characterized by division and competition as any other complex bureaucratic apparatus.

There is certainly no widespread support for the proposal made on one campus to integrate all institutional studies conducted on campus in a single office under the direction of an administrative vice-president for research and information. Quite often, in fact, research units have tended to multiply as campuses have grown in size. Shortly after his appointment the dean of liberal arts at one university indicated his intention to bypass the university's bureau of institutional research and to rely on his own research operation for studies related to his needs. The effect of his decision was to counteract the trend toward the centralization of information —and administrative power—in the IR office.

Contrasting approaches to the organization of institutional self-study can be found at the neighboring universities of Washington and Oregon. At the University of Washington most of the administrative units do their own research and analysis, and a small office known as the Office of Institutional Educational Research confines itself mostly to studies of student characteristics and performance. The registrar, the business office, the planning office, and several other agencies share, in effect, the responsibility for conducting research into the institution's operations. This decentralization of the research function prevents any single office from gaining a monopoly of critical information and fosters an analytical attitude toward their own activities by operating agencies. The president prefers this arrangement because, as he puts it, he wants to have his line departments "research-minded." At the same time, of course, this decentralized structure poses problems with respect to the duplication of effort, which has forced these decentralized agencies to develop informal means of co-ordinating their activities.

At the University of Oregon institutional research is carried on by the office of the Director of Institutional Planning and Research. The title of the office suggests the broad range of the director's responsibility. He studies long-range growth problems of the university, curriculum development (such as the question of introducing new Ph. D. programs), and general sociological and psychological problems of the campus community (such as the role of women students and their influence on the university). In addition, the office gathers general data concerning costs, space, and university organization. Even with this concentration of institutional research in one office at the University of Oregon, several other agencies continue to do their own studies to complement the work of the central office. What the Oregon example suggests is that the presence of a highly developed IR office will not necessarily pre-empt the research functions of other university agencies but may instead represent a net increase in the amount of research conducted on the campus.

A persistent problem underlying a multi-centered system for conducting research is the difficulty of getting all agencies to consent to the free exchange of data. At one institution the president's secretary jealously guarded all the career data in her files on faculty members, and it took a direct order from the president before she would consent to share her records with the institutional research agency. The agency needed this information for a study it was conducting of the academic backgrounds of faculty members.

Barriers of this kind to the free flow of information are common. In part they merely reflect the defense of jurisdictional prerogatives. Knowledge is an aspect of administrative power which agencies are as reluctant to share as they are any other attribute of their sovereignty. But there are other concerns here as well, not the least of which is the embarrassing effects, already noted, that certain kinds of disclosures may have. A school or department within a university can hardly be expected to relish the prospect of having wide publicity given to certain disadvantageous information about itself including, for example, the fact that it has succeeded in attracting only a very small number of talented students to its Ph.D. program. The circulation of certain kinds of information is therefore subject to very careful internal safeguards within some institutions.

Even more anxiety may be felt over the disclosure of sensitive information to the outside world. At one midwestern university the institutional research agency conducted a study of student expenditures on campus. It found cases in which students were spending as much as $7,000 annually during their academic careers (although average expenditures were considerably less). These findings were extremely discomforting to the president, who for years had been warding off legislative efforts to raise tuition at his institution with the claim that the university was primarily a place where the economically underprivileged children of the state could obtain an education. It was only after considerable discussion, and after strong pressure had been exerted by the advisory committee on institutional research, that the president consented to have a somewhat amended report released for publication.

The extent of the restrictions imposed on the release of IR studies is shown in Table 3–2. Noteworthy here is the fact that only 3 per cent of all the schools surveyed followed a clearly "open" policy with respect to institutional research, distributing studies freely to either the internal staff or the public at large. All other institutions imposed at least partial restrictions on the circulation of institutional research reports.

Among IR directors themselves opinion is sharply divided over the advisability of restricting the circulation of their reports, as Table 3–3 indicates. One director summed up the view of many of his colleagues in these terms: "Most studies require some professional experience and skill to interpret properly. It is difficult to educate a public or an individual predisposed to misuse any and all information to the detriment of the institution. It is important to recognize that a goal of many internal studies is to identify weaknesses so that they may be corrected." Another argument presented against releasing certain data to the outside world was that much

TABLE 3–2: THE CIRCULATION OF INSTITUTIONAL RESEARCH REPORTS

Policies Governing Distribution of IR Studies	No. of Schools	% (n = 128)
Controlled by administration	49	38
Controlled by initiators of study	24	19
Depends on purpose and content of study	16	13
Controlled by faculty	10	8
No established policy	9	7
Whatever seems appropriate	6	5
All studies released to general public	3	2
Distributed to entire staff	2	1
Other [a]	9	7
Totals	128	100

[a] This category includes institutions which did not answer this item as well as responses which were not classifiable.

TABLE 3-3: THE SENSITIVITY OF INSTITUTIONAL RESEARCH: ATTITUDES OF IR DIRECTORS TOWARD THE PUBLIC RELEASE OF THEIR STUDIES

Attitudes of IR Directors	No. of Schools	% (n = 128)
Would cause major controversy	48	37
Would *not* cause major controversy	42	33
Too early to judge	6	5
Qualified affirmative	11	9
No opinion [a]	21	16
Totals	128	100

[a] This category includes institutions which did not answer this item as well as responses which were not classifiable.

of it is only of "limited, local interest, done for a particular person or group." Anticipating an unfriendly reception by hostile critics in the external environment, some directors feel that studies should not be released until they can be accompanied by "complete" explanations.

There were a good many directors, however, who were prepared to accept whatever risks a policy of disclosure might entail. As one director put it, "the institutional studies are valuable in revealing the causes of our failure and success and the needs which the public and the legislature can help meet with appropriations and other support. The studies also convince the accrediting associations of our excellence as a college." But still another director argued that while he did not feel release of findings would stir up controversy, he was convinced that "publication of data dealing with similar activities always elicits comparison," which "is not always in the best interest of the concerned institution. Each institution in many respects is and should be considered as unique."

In states in which a number of state institutions of higher education must compete for funds, each institution may be pressed to develop data that will justify the largest possible allocation of funds to the home campus. And in states which use formulas as a means of distributing legislative appropriations among the state institutions, institutional research is likely to be thrown into the contest to determine the ground rules for the allocation formula. A university with large graduate enrollments, in which the graduate student carries an average of eight or ten hours in contrast to the fifteen-hour load of undergraduates, can be expected to resist to the end any move to define a full-time student as one who carries a fifteen-hour load, particularly when this definition becomes the basis for allocating the annual appropriation for higher education. So the institutional research of the university will be geared to proving the case against a flat fifteen-hour formula. In this context institutional research is not so much a tool of internal management as it is an instrument for controlling the external environment.

TABLE 3–4: STATE CO-ORDINATING AGENCIES AND INSTITUTIONAL RESEARCH

Is there a central co-ordinating agency in your state which conducts institutional research?	No. of Schools	% (n = 128)
Yes	63	49
No	52	40
No reply	13	11
Totals	128	100

TABLE 3–5: THE GROWING ROLE OF STATE CO-ORDINATING AGENCIES IN INSTITUTIONAL RESEARCH

Question: Is the legislature showing an increasing tendency to look to central co-ordinating bodies for basic data on the performance of individual institutions?

	Yes	No	Divided Opinion[a]
	Arkansas	Connecticut	Colorado
	California	Kentucky	Florida
	Illinois	Minnesota	Massachusetts
	Indiana	Mississippi	Michigan
	Iowa	New York	Wisconsin
	Kansas	Pennsylvania	
	Missouri	South Dakota	
	Montana	Washington	
	New Jersey		
	New Mexico		
	Ohio		
	Oklahoma		
	Oregon		
	Rhode Island		
	South Carolina		
	Tennessee		
	Texas		
	Utah		
	Virginia		
Total	19	8	5
% (n = 32)	59	25	16

[a] In these cases of divided opinion some of the institutions in the state replying to the question indicated their belief that the legislature was showing a tendency to look to central co-ordinating bodies for institutional research, while others held there was no such tendency.

In such competitive states the legislature may well assign the task of institutional research to a central co-ordinating body not connected with any of the individual schools in the hope that a neutral agency will come up with a more objective basis for allocating funds. Nearly 50 per cent of all the schools in our survey reported that there is a co-ordinating agency in their state which conducts institutional research (see Table 3–4). Moreover, a large number of these schools indicated that the legislature was showing an increasing tendency to look to this central office for basic data on the performance of individual schools (see Table 3–5). In Michigan, for example, the central co-ordinating body has begun to play an increasingly active role in planning and carrying on statewide studies of costs and other matters in collaboration with the individual institutions. Once this development occurs, however, the institutions may turn their energies to convincing the central research agency of the merits of their local campus data. The arena of conflict may be shifted, but the dispute among institutions is certainly not resolved.

THE INFLUENCE OF INSTITUTIONAL RESEARCH

As yet it is far from clear what effect institutional research will ultimately have upon university policy and planning at the institutions at which it is being conducted. At the University of Rhode Island it could fairly be said when this survey was made that the bureau of institutional research and its director were at the right hand of the president and at the center of university decision making. In fact the president of the university has gone on record as believing that the IR director should be "a close adviser of the president" and that no administrator should exercise more influence over the chief executive of a university. Indeed, he argues that the position of institutional research director "is an excellent training ground for presidential aspirants."[6]

The office of institutional research at Northern Illinois University is in a similarly strong position. The director of the bureau reports directly to the president, who relies heavily upon the advice of the agency in the formation of university policy. A great many of the key decisions made at Northern Illinois in the past five years have resulted directly from studies conducted by the institutional research unit. The bureau director represents the university in statewide planning meetings, and the agency he heads has long since moved beyond the role of a purely fact-gathering office into the task of defining basic university goals.

But Rhode Island and Northern Illinois illustrate maximum possibilities

[6] See the address by the president of the university in Lins, *The Role of Institutional Planning*, p. 12.

open to an IR office rather than the typical situation. It is more characteristic for such an office to serve in a staff capacity and for its director to be at most a technical consultant to the top levels of university policy making. And there are still some universities where institutional research is isolated from the center of policy, its studies largely ignored by university administrators and without apparent influence on their decisions. There is a story, perhaps apocryphal, that the president of one southern university hired a professional consultant to conduct a study of his institution's operations only to discover that he already had a bureau of institutional research on his campus specifically charged with responsibility for this kind of project. It was certainly clear in a great many of our interviews that university presidents put a somewhat lower estimate upon the role of IR directors in making university policy than do the directors themselves.

The closer a bureau of institutional research is to the president's office, the more immediate and direct its influence on university policy is likely to be. Hence the preferred position of institutional research at Rhode Island and Northern Illinois has considerable appeal in some quarters. Our questionnaire asked each institutional research director if he saw himself as being a "right-hand man" to the president. As Table 3–6 reveals, a substantial majority of IR directors did see their role in precisely this way, while a great many others gave qualified answers which indicated at least partial agreement with this proposition.

TABLE 3–6: SHOULD AN INSTITUTIONAL RESEARCH DIRECTOR BECOME A UNIVERSITY PRESIDENT'S "RIGHT-HAND MAN"?

Attitude of Director	No. of Schools	% (n = 128)
Agree	60	47
Disagree	17	14
Depends on nature and size of institution and the role of the office	12	9
Should be *one* of the right-hand men	9	7
Depends on the individual and/or president's decision	3	2
If responsible for implementing—no; for formulating—yes	5	4
Other[a]	22	17
Totals	128	100

[a] This category includes institutions which did not answer this item as well as responses which were not classifiable.

The problem that arises, however, is that a university is a dual organization in which control over decision making is shared between administrators and academicians. To the extent that an office of institutional research becomes identified as an arm of administrative authority it loses some of its persuasive capacity with the academic departments. The dean of arts and sciences at one institution contended that the office of instutitional research should scrupulously avoid any identification with the administration and should cultivate instead a reputation for neutrality and independence on the local campus akin to that of the U.S. Bureau of Labor Statistics on the national scene. Only in this way, he argued, would the findings of an IR agency have any substantial influence with the faculty.

At another university the institutional research director took the position that his office should enjoy a degree of independence sufficient to allow him to disagree with the president if the occasion demanded such dissent. Recently, he pointed out, the president had declared himself very strongly in favor of the establishment of an African language program at the university, whereupon the IR director took it upon himself to write a sharp letter of protest against this proposal. In this letter he pointed out to the president that his attitude with respect to African languages was inconsistent with the university's general effort to cut down on the proliferation of courses for which the IR office had shown there was only a limited student demand. Of course the director's ability to write such a letter was enormously facilitated by the fact that he had been engaged in institutional research activity on campus for more than two decades, and over this period he had acquired a reputation and standing which made him a powerful figure in his own right in the university community.

It is frequently pointed out that many of the questions investigated through institutional research at individual universities today have already been answered by studies conducted on other campuses. Such duplication is, of course, widespread, but it is to a very large extent inevitable. In the system of higher education which prevails in this country each institution tends to regard itself as having a very distinctive set of goals which set it apart from other educational organizations. To be sure, this conception is to some extent an illusion, since American universities tend, as David Riesman points out, to be isomorphic in character[7]—to imitate each other in their purposes and organizational procedures. But the belief of educators in the uniqueness of their own institutions is a strong one, and it represents a substantial barrier against efforts to apply the findings of an institutional research project conducted in one campus setting to answer questions raised in another.

[7] See David Riesman, *Constraint and Variety in American Education* (New York: Doubleday Anchor, 1958), pp. 10–11.

Hence many of the studies undertaken in the name of institutional research today are not so much designed to answer questions as they are to win support for findings which administrators know about from reports published by other schools and which they hope to see applied to their own campuses. As one IR director put it, "The situation is that each institution group, whether faculty or administration, feels the need to be convinced on its own ground."[8] While the ideology of institutional research thus stresses its importance as a "basis for decision,"[9] in actual practice such research also serves as a means of implementing courses of action already decided upon. In this context institutional research becomes part of a strategy aimed at overcoming resistance to change. It is an instrument in the hands of the decision maker rather than a source of decision.

Our questionnaire asked institutional research directors themselves to classify their office as either a "basic data-gathering agency" or a "participant in major university decisions." Table 3–7 presents the response of IR directors to this item. While a preponderance of directors see their office as playing a data-gathering role, the comments of IR directors on this question suggest wide agreement on their part that data gathering itself has substantial policy implications. Witness, for example, the following statement from a director who claimed only a fact-finding function for his office: "Basically, the proper function of institutional research is fact-finding. Fact-finding and policy decision-making are not, however, mutually exclusive. Consciously or unconsciously, even the most scrupulously objective researcher influences the reaction to his findings."

Those directors of institutional research who identified participation in top-level decision making as the major function of their office did not disparage fact-gathering activity in their replies. Rather they saw it as only

[8] *Conference on Institutional Research in Higher Education*, p. 23.

[9] See the collection of papers on institutional research edited by L. Joseph Lins, *Basis for Decision* (Madison, Wis.: Dembar Educational Research Services, Inc., 1963).

TABLE 3–7: INSTITUTIONAL RESEARCH AS SEEN BY IR DIRECTORS

Major Role of IR Agency according to IR Director	No. of Schools	% (n = 128)
A basic data-gathering agency	55	43
A participant in major university decision making	24	20
Both	33	26
No opinion[a]	16	11
Totals	128	100

[a] This category includes institutions which did not answer this item as well as responses which were not classifiable.

a partial dimension, even if an important aspect of their work. One such director put it this way: "Gathering facts for their own sake is senseless. The facts must be evaluated so that sound decisions can be made. This office does not make decisions. It collects, analyzes, reports, and sometimes recommends. I feel this makes me a participant in major university decisions."

As a method of tracing the impact of institutional research upon policy making, IR directors were also asked if they presented policy recommendations to university executives along with their reports or if they let their findings speak for themselves. Table 3–8 presents the views of directors on this score. The comments of directors as well as the returns in Table 3–8 point up the fact that almost half of the directors feel a clear responsibility to submit policy recommendations along with their research findings. Illustrative of this attitude was the following: "You can never let 'findings speak for themselves' because people read the evidence in too many different ways. There are always interpretational cautions which must accompany data . . . more important, a suggestion usually stimulates a reaction, or more thinking as to the best direction to follow."

Even those directors who do not feel obligated to make specific policy recommendations nonetheless feel that their role does entail the interpretation of data, including the identification of trends, indication of the outcomes of possible courses of action, and even the listing of a number of policy alternatives among which university executives may choose. A typical expression of this attitude was the following comment: "I suspect that, in the limited areas in which my findings bear upon educational policy, I do not hesitate to point out the implications of the data, and to

TABLE 3–8: MANNER IN WHICH IR DIRECTOR REPORTS FINDINGS TO UNIVERSITY OFFICIALS

Alternative Roles of IR Directors	No. of Schools	% (n = 128)
Make policy recommendations to university executives along with his reports	53	41
Let his findings speak for themselves	43	34
Cannot be separated in practice	10	8
Qualified answers (e.g., depends on the nature of the study)	9	7
Other[a]	13	10
Totals	128	100

[a] This category includes institutions which did not answer this item as well as responses which were not classifiable.

suggest what I think ought to be done about it. It sometimes has an effect and sometimes doesn't." Very much in the minority are those directors who contend that their role should be strictly confined to the presentation of facts, without interpretation or recommendation: "This office takes the position that university executives can recognize trends from the reports and studies submitted to them. For this office to make policy recommendations would infer that the university executives were not capable of responding to the 'handwriting on the wall.' "

Whatever the view of IR directors may be on their role in educational administration, it is actually very difficult to assess the real effects of institutional research on university decision making. One item in our questionnaire asked IR directors what, if any, major steps or changes in the university's policy or development in recent years had directly resulted from the work of their office. Most of the directors who responded to this item (and a great many left it blank) indicated the difficulty of demonstrating the impact of this sort of research upon policy decisions or outcomes. The following is typical of the general response: "This is virtually impossible to answer. Our cost studies have affected the decisions of the University Budget Committee. (The director of the Office for Institutional Research serves as a consultant to the Budget Committee and participates in the budget hearings.) Studies of salaries have influenced the decision of the university to seek much larger appropriations from the Legislature for salaries, but I cannot be positive that this same thing would not have happened if the Office of Institutional Research had not conducted salary studies." Another IR director described the role of institutional research at his university in these terms: "IR works as part of the President's office as a staff aid to him and others on the campus. We feel that many things are different because we are here lending an objective view to the process of running a university."

PROSPECTS FOR THE FUTURE

If the trends manifest over the past decade continue their present course, there can be little doubt that in years to come research into their own operations will become an increasingly common characteristic of public institutions of higher education in this country. The pressures from the external environment, particularly from the offices and agencies of state government, will be as important as any other factor in stimulating this development. As booming enrollments force the costs of higher education constantly upward, a growing number of state legislators and executive officials will ask questions which will require college and university officials to provide more refined data about their own operations. The expanded involvement of the federal government in higher education will undoubtedly have the same effect for private as well as public institutions. For defensive reasons alone, institutions of higher education will thus be pushed into conducting studies designed to obtain precise data on the efficiency with which they are being managed.

If present trends continue, the growth of such institutional self-study will take place in a number of directions and under the auspices of a variety of university offices and agencies. There was no evidence from our survey that formally designated offices of institutional research are tending to acquire anything resembling a monopoly of the research function as far as campus operations are concerned. Offices of fiscal analysis, planning units, registrar's offices—these and a number of other agencies continue to conduct quantitative studies of management problems along with IR offices. That this presents problems of co-ordination is clear. In the future as in the past, universities may find themselves embarrassed by the fact that two of their research offices are issuing different figures to the press on enrollment projections or some other topic of pressing public concern. The possibility of such duplication can be reduced by the establishment of a co-ordinating mechanism on campus, such as a committee representative of all the agencies engaged in the study of institutional operations. This practice is now followed at Michigan State and the University of Washington, and it certainly seems worthy of imitation by other universities.

Most institutions seem prepared to live with a plural arrangement for self-study, even when it means duplication of effort or the occasional possibility that an institution may appear to speak with two voices. In part this tolerance of diversity springs from the decentralized structure of power in university administration, which places formidable difficulties in the path of any attempt to integrate jurisdiction over the study of all aspects of university operations in one office. But it has also been noted that there is no push from institutional research directors themselves to gain a monopoly of control over research. Most IR directors appear to accept a limited conception of their own research function within the university. And an effort to combine all management research in one office would require the creation of a cumbersome administrative structure for such self-study, one that would be top-heavy and unwieldy.

As IR directors have begun to define their role at many of the larger universities, there is growing agreement that an institutional research office as such can have a clear and distinct mission on campus. This mission lies in the development of the office as an arm of academic administration, providing information relevant to the problems that arise on the agenda of deans and academic vice-presidents at the larger institutions, or on the academic side of a college president's responsibilities at the smaller schools. As its primary responsibility such an office collects and analyzes information bearing on the effectiveness with which a college or university is achieving its academic goals.

This conception of an institutional research office sets it distinctly apart from the business side of university operations. Under this arrangement, management problems connected with student registration, employee payrolls, and the utilization of physical facilities are not the responsibility of the office of institutional research. Jurisdiction over the housekeeping side of university administration rests instead with the vice-president for finance, the registrar, the plant manager's office, or is divided among a number of these campus agencies.

The attention of the IR office with an academic orientation is rather centered on such matters as innovations in degree programs, the background and quality of the student body, and the recruitment and retention of a top-flight academic staff. It thus has the task of shoring up with data the most difficult and elusive side of university decision, that pertaining to the academic development of the institution. While serving as an instrument of academic administration, such an office must work closely and sympathetically with the various faculties, perhaps through the mechanism of a faculty advisory committee. In time an institutional research office of this sort can become a vital force bolstering the point of view of the faculty in decisions which involve simultaneously a combination of academic as well as business needs and resources. Moreover, such an institutional research office can provide invaluable assistance to an academic vice-president in his efforts to advance and protect the interests of faculty and students in the development of university policy. One academic vice-president commented that without the supporting data provided by an office of institutional research he would not be able to match the influence exerted by the vice-president for business affairs at the highest levels of university decision making.

As was noted in Chapter 1, management research in universities as in other organizations very often tends to be centered on costs rather than achievements, on inputs rather than outputs. An IR office with an academic orientation can focus attention instead on the goals of a university and the need to subordinate all other concerns to the achievement of academic objectives, rather than, as is often the case, fashioning academic goals merely to capitalize on the availability of resources.

As part of its role this kind of office of institutional research can also be a clearing house for information about the experience of other institutions and educational experiments being conducted elsewhere that may be relevant to its own school. If the IR office is located near the president, or under an academic vice-president, its findings are more likely to be injected into the mainstream of the decision-making process on educational policy. And in the last analysis, institutional research can only justify itself through its contribution to the choices a university must make about its academic development.

Moreover, the personnel and informational facilities of the office of institutional research can also be made available to faculty committees and departments involved in the study of academic problems at the university. In this way the presence of an IR office on campus can stimulate the individual departments and academic groups to engage in a good deal more self-study and evaluation than has traditionally been the case. In any event, it is the function of an academically oriented institutional research agency to encourage the study of academic problems by other groups on campus and not to monopolize this function for itself. The personnel of the office of institutional research can even serve, as at Minnesota, in a staff capacity to other study groups on campus.

If it is to be successful, an IR office must obtain the co-operation of the registrar's office, the deans of the various schools, and other university agencies which may have information relevant to the study of academic problems. A close relationship with the registrar's office will be particularly important for the success of the institutional research operation, since the basic data on student background and performance originate in the registrar's office. The IR office can also lend assistance to the deans and development officials responsible for obtaining financial support from state legislatures, foundations, and agencies of the federal government.

In order to preserve its academic orientation, it is vitally important that an institutional research agency not become extensively involved in studies of costs, space utilization, or other areas of university operations not immediately related to academic programs. If it is preoccupied with studies of this sort, it will have little time or energy left for its primary mission—the study of academic programs and policies at the university. At the same time, however, the study of costs and analysis of the use of physical facilities have become major sources of managerial innovation in higher education today. In the chapter that follows, the effect upon university management of changes in each of these areas is subject to detailed examination.

Chapter Four

ALLOCATING ACADEMIC RESOURCES

Two areas of university operation—budgeting and space management— have been prime targets for the managerial revolution in higher education. As essential resources for any academic institution, money and physical facilities are invariably studied, argued over, and sought after by educators. And as measurable factors in the educational process, money and space can be subject to the quantification and objective analysis of modern management somewhat more easily than can the achievement of a student or the performance of a professor.

Three observations stand out in our study of the allocation of resources. First, there is an unmistakable trend toward more rationalized procedures in the management of money and space, notably in the increasing use of formulas, cost analyses, and new methods of displaying fiscal and space data. Secondly, these rationalized procedures are primarily applied to larger aggregates of resources, especially where statewide budgets must be divided among individual institutions. Within smaller units of operation, such as an individual department or a college of arts and sciences, resource allocation tends to remain highly subjective. Finally, while the content of decisions may not always be altered, there seems to be little doubt that the new techniques have changed the locale of important policy decisions, often shifting effective control from one hierarchical level of administration to another, or laterally from one group of officials to another, as for example, from deans to business officers.

Although budgeting and space management have been exposed to many of the same developments, significant differences in the two areas make it appropriate to divide our discussion of resource allocation at this point, taking up budgeting first, space management next, and concluding with an analysis of similarities and differences between these two salient areas of managerial innovation in higher education.

THE NEW PHILOSOPHY OF BUDGETING

The budget of an academic institution is both a technical instrument of management and a policy document which reflects changes taking place in the academic direction of an institution. The important changes in budgetary theory and practice which have occurred in the postwar years have influenced both aspects of university budgeting. Indeed, a technical change in budget format, which on the surface appears to be little more than a routine revision in the housekeeping procedures of an institution, may have subtle and far-reaching effects on the destinies of certain university programs. Conversely, decisions regarding the allocation of university resources may sometimes be made without regard for meticulously arranged budget procedures. This relationship between the technical side of budgeting and the policy implications of the budgetary process will be of prime interest in this analysis.

The Program Budget

On the technical side, the principal change in budgetary practice in higher education—as in government agencies and private industry—has been a conversion from old-style object or line-item budgets to a new system of program budgeting. Our survey showed that three-fourths of American state colleges and universities now employ some form of program budget, while only a fourth still use a strict object budget (and a number of these report that they plan to convert to program budgeting in the near future).

Essentially the object budget reveals only the items for which checks are written to pay the bills. At the University of Maine, for example, the principal classifications in the budget are salaries and wages, materials and supplies, other current expense, maintenance and alterations, capital outlay, travel, and interdepartmental credits.[1] Such a budget is a useful record of the outlays of the institution but indicates virtually nothing about the way in which money is being spent to achieve the major goals of the institution. The program budget, by contrast, is an effort to arrange the budget according to institutional purposes or programs. A reader of the budget can identify at a glance the principal objectives of the institution and the amount of money assigned to each area. The mammoth budget of the University of California system which stood at over $300,000,000 for 1966–67, is displayed in programmatic terms in Figure 4–1.

A majority of the institutions in our survey actually make use of a format which mixes object and program categories. This mixture usually means that the program categories are the major units of classification within the total budget, while expenditures for each program are broken down according to object categories. In a program called "research," for

[1] The University of Maine is one of the few institutions in the country which has switched away from program budgets back to object budgets.

FIGURE 4–1

UNIVERSITY OF CALIFORNIA, BUDGET FOR CURRENT OPERATIONS, 1966–1967

THE 1966–67 BUDGET DOLLAR

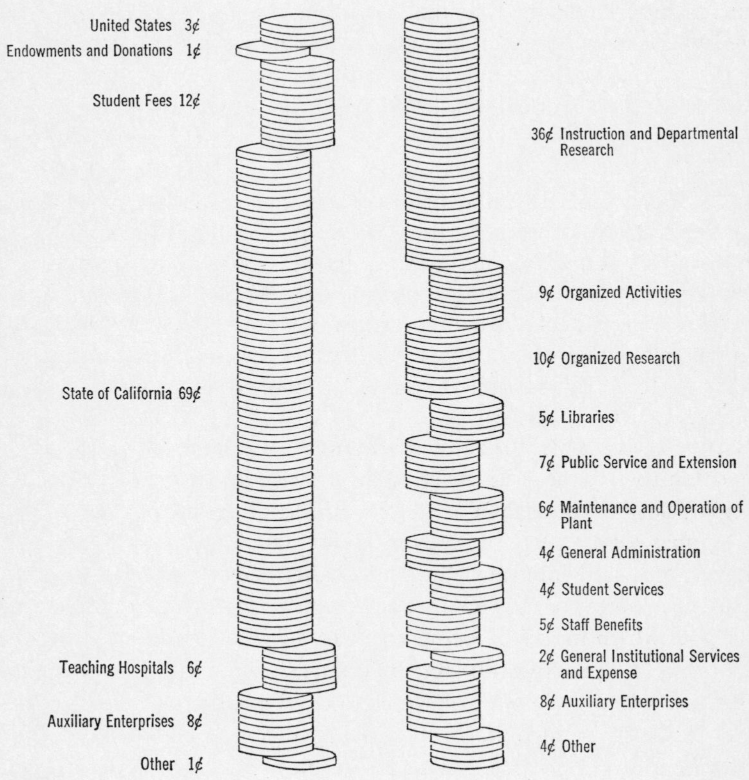

Note: Budget illustration provided by the courtesy of the University of California's Office of Business and Finance.

example, the Oregon State System of Higher Education works out subtotals for salaries and wages, services and supplies, and capital outlay. Many universities organize their budgets in several different ways at once. The University of Colorado presents a budget to the legislature with its requests arranged first by program, then by object, and finally in a combination of these two systems.[2]

Modern program budgeting was developed initially outside of higher education. Early forms of program budgeting appeared in municipal governments at the beginning of the twentieth century. Although the Taft Commission on Economy and Efficiency showed an interest in budgetary reform as early as 1912, the national government itself made little headway in program budgeting until the 1930's, when the Tennessee Valley Authority and the U.S. Department of Agriculture pioneered with program formats.[3] The first Hoover Commission in 1949 called for the use of a "performance budget" in all government agencies,[4] a recommendation which has been largely carried out in the national government. State governments have also moved toward program budgeting, although a number of states have clung tenaciously to the line-item system, creating important cross pressures on the budgeting procedures of public institutions of higher education, which will be discussed shortly.[5]

One single source, however, has exerted a profound influence on the specific character of most college and university budgets. This is the model budgeting procedure developed by the American Council on Education, whose standard work, *College and University Business Administration*, Vol. I, has been the prototype for academic budgeting in American educational institutions since its publication in 1952. Not all colleges and universities acknowledge their debt to the American Council system, but among institutions using program budgets there is a striking similarity to the A.C.E. model. Under "educational and general expenditures" the American Council suggested eight program categories: general administration, general expense, instructional and departmental research, organized activities relating to educational departments, organized research, extension and public services, libraries, and operation and maintenance of physical plant. These categories have now become household words in university business offices.

[2] See, as examples, University of California, *Budget for Current Operations, 1964–65;* Oregon State System of Higher Education, *Biennial Budget, 1963–65;* and University of Colorado, *1964–65 Request Budget.*

[3] Jesse Burkhead, *Government Budgeting* (New York: John Wiley, 1956), pp. 133–39, reviews the development of program budgeting in government agencies.

[4] Commission on Organization of the Executive Branch of the Government, *Budgeting and Accounting* (Washington: U.S. Government Printing Office, 1949), p. 8. The terms "program budgeting" and "performance budgeting" are often used interchangeably. In some budgetary literature, however, the term "performance budgeting" signifies a still more advanced form of program budgeting in which actual standards of expected performance are established within budget programs.

[5] For a general summary of state budgeting procedures in the United States, see Council of State Governments, *The Book of the States, 1964–65* (Chicago: Council of State Governments, 1964), pp. 153–67.

The A.C.E. volume also set forth suggested reporting and accounting procedures which are matched to the main program categories of the model budget. This handbook, along with a companion volume on other business activities, was virtually the only recognized reference work available to all colleges and universities for more than a decade, and it can be found on the desk of almost every academic business officer today. Repeatedly, in interviews and in responses to questionnaires, university officials identified the American Council model as the inspiration for their own internal budgeting procedure.

New Instruments of Analysis

The transition from object budgets to program budgets has been paralleled by the development of new techniques of cost analysis, formula budgeting, and intricate systems of reporting and requesting funds. While the concept of the program budget has been the focal point of contemporary budget theory, these related budgetary practices have played an equally important role in the development of modern budgeting techniques. The program budget mainly establishes the format; it does not give the budget officer the instruments of analysis which are necessary to power the budgetary process.

The chief problem which confronts all budgetary analysis has been clearly stated by Verne Lewis: "On what basis shall it be decided to allocate X dollars to Activity A instead of allocating them to Activity B, or instead of allowing the taxpayer to use the money for his individual purposes?"[6] For even with a stylish format and modern techniques of reporting and display, those with the responsibility for budgetary decisions are still faced with the problem of deciding what to spend money on. Fiscal analysts have thus been tantalized with the thought of developing a budgetary science through which the "best" decision could be made on the basis of "hard data" and clearly specified goals. This has given rise to a new surge of interest in cost-benefit analysis, marginal utility, and goal setting—concepts borrowed or adapted from economic theory—as devices for the establishment of an objective science of budgetary decision making. To put these concepts into operational form, computers have been employed to program complete models of an agency so that inputs and outputs in the budgetary process can be analyzed with greater precision.

Compared to General Motors or the U.S. Department of Defense academic institutions have not yet made very extensive use of high

[6] Verne B. Lewis, "Toward a Theory of Budgeting," *Public Administration Review* XII (Winter, 1952), 42.

powered techniques of budgetary analysis. But along with changes in their budget structure, state colleges and universities have begun to employ several techniques of analysis associated with modern budgeting, most notably budgeting formulas and quantitative cost analysis. Eighty-one per cent of the state institutions responding to our questionnaire now use some kind of formula in the preparation of their budgets (see Table 4–1). And two-thirds of the institutions have begun to use quantitative cost analysis (see Table 4–2).

In practice, the terms "cost analysis" and "formula" are sometimes blurred and frequently used interchangeably, since both formulas and cost analysis are means of quantifying the expenditure pattern of an institution or agency. There are, however, important differences. As one writer has suggested, " a budget formula and a cost analysis procedure differ principally in that cost analysis is designed to measure cost-program relationships which already exist, either in the form of actual past or present expenditures, whereas a budget formula is designed to form the basis for an estimate of future budgetary requirements through the use of

TABLE 4–1: QUANTITATIVE FORMULAS USED IN BUDGET PREPARATION

Type of Formula	No. of Schools	% (n = 259)
Student-faculty ratio	180	70
Faculty staffing formulas	126	49
Staffing formulas for nonacademic personnel	85	33
Distribution of students among divisions	69	27
Operations and maintenance	5	2
None	48	19

TABLE 4–2: AREAS SUBJECT TO COST ANALYSIS IN BUDGET PREPARATION

Area	No. of Schools	% (n = 259)
Instructional costs	141	54
Central Services costs (motor pool, etc.)	88	34
Admissions	15	6
Registration	14	5
Payroll	14	5
None	89	34

predetermined program-cost relationships coupled with estimates of futur levels of program activity."[7]

Cost analysis, in other words, measures the unit cost of past an present operations. At Florida State University, for example, instructiona costs are calculated in considerable detail. A report on that institution' operations in 1962–63 showed that the lower-division general universit expenditure for instruction in the classics department was $297 per ful time-equivalent student, while the classroom teaching salary cost i classics was $795 per full-time-equivalent student. In the graduate divisio of the classics department the average salary rate per FTE teacher wa $6,655, and in the upper division of the same department the rate wa $7,237 per FTE teacher.[8]

A budget formula, on the other hand, is primarily a means of estimatin future expenditures. Academic institutions in New Mexico use studen faculty ratios, formulas for the distribution of students among division and staffing formulas in budget planning. Most frequently, budg formulas use fixed and accepted quantities, such as a 15-to-1 studen faculty ratio. With certain modifications, these ratios become the bas for calculating the appropriation requests submitted by the New Mexic institutions of higher education to the legislature.

The Boundaries of Budgeting

Formulas, cost analysis, and program budgeting have become so co monplace in higher education that a casual observer could easily assun that a genuine science of budgeting had indeed replaced the rule-of-thum procedures of earlier days. Quite emphatically, this is not the case. O own analysis of budgetary practice suggests that several major restrai still restrict the use of modern budgeting in academic institutions:

1. *Problems of quantification and objective analysis, which are centr to modern budgetary theory, are far from being solved in higher educati* The main work of academic institutions—the education of students a the advancement of knowledge—can at present be subject only to t grossest kinds of measurement. A simple head count of graduating stude or of the array of articles in a professor's bibliography is scarcely

[7] James L. Miller, Jr., *State Budgeting for Higher Education: The Use of Form and Cost Analysis* (Ann Arbor, Mich.: Institute of Public Administration, 1964), p. Miller goes on to note, "In the case of cost analysis, the gross measures of both progr and cost are known factors and the relationship between them is the unknown fact In the case of a formula, the known factors are future program level (estimated) and program-cost relationship (predetermined), and the unknown factor is the future t cost."

[8] *An Analysis of Factors Related to the Operation of the Florida State Univers 1962–1963* (Tallahassee: Office of Institutional Research and Service, Florida S University, mimeo., 1964), p. 6.

adequate measure of whether an institution is achieving its educational goals. Certain areas of institutional activity can be subjected to such measurement—for example, the number of meals served in the student cafeteria—but these operations are among the least important activities of the institution.

Where direct measurements cannot be applied with confidence, but where some kind of measurement is still demanded, university officials are forced to indirect measures, with all of their attendant problems. The number of hours a student or a professor spends in class measures very little about academic performance, but yardsticks such as the student credit-hour and the full-time-equivalent workload have been widely employed as indirect measures of otherwise immeasurable activities.[9] As a result of using such quantification, however, a university runs the risk that its indirect measures will acquire greater influence than they really deserve.

2. *In addition to the problems of measurement in higher education, long-standing traditions in academic life restrict the application of rigorous budgetary procedures.* Except in unusual circumstances, it has long been customary in academic circles to give each department at least as much as it received in the previous budget. This amount is the base, or starting point, for most budgetary deliberations, and it is only rarely that the merits of this base budget can be successfully questioned. The tenure system of appointment and promotion further insulates the base from annual reappraisal, since the tenured professors cannot ordinarily be dislodged from their positions except by death or retirement. But in practice the legal force of tenure appears to be no more important in defending the base of a department's budget than the widespread acceptance by the academic community of the idea that no department should be cut below its existing level of support.

A second tradition which offers resistance to rationalized budgeting is the idea of equity in resource allocation. It is difficult, for example, for an administrator to authorize a new position for the department of history without facing the argument that he is now required to authorize similar positions in the other social science departments. Similarly it is often

[9] Miller, *State Budgeting for Higher Education*, deals with the problem of indirect measurement: "When direct measurement is not possible, there are two methods of indirect measurement which can be used: (1) indirect measurement by evaluating the methods employed, and (2) indirect measurement by evaluating the results achieved. The former is applicable when there is some general agreement on the 'best' methods for achieving the intended outcome and those methods are measurable in some kind of units even though the outcome itself is not. . . . Indirect measurement by evaluating the results achieved is applicable when the ultimate results are measurable in unit terms." (p. 76).

difficult for a faculty council to recommend the promotion of one professor without being strongly pressured to recommend the promotion of a dozen more in roughly similar circumstances. It is no exaggeration to say that every "emergency" promotion which is made to keep a faculty member from leaving for another institution may trigger two or three other promotions in order to adhere to the standard of equity among departments.[10]

Since budgeting penetrates every area of institutional life, any proposal which threatens the base of departments or violates the concept of fair shares is likely to encounter opposition from individual departments. Other management innovations—in institutional research, information systems, or in the administrative use of computers—can often be added to the existing administrative scheme without upsetting established arrangements. Budgetary innovation, on the other hand, poses an immediate and highly visible threat to existing patterns of financial support for departmental activities. And while there is, in fact, little evidence that modifications in budgeting procedures actually produce shifts in the allocation of resources, academicians are more uneasy about budgetary changes than any other phase of management innovation. The mere possibility of damage to the base of a department is enough to create resistance. The fact that innovations have occurred, and with such rapidity, is in fact remarkable in view of the tensions involved. Our impression is that the innovations have been tolerated mainly because they have not yet had a major effect on allocation decisions in universities and have been used primarily as a means of protecting the over-all base of support for the university—points which we shall discuss shortly.

3. *The conditions of the modern academic market place also make it difficult to adhere to rationalized techniques in administering the budget.* With universities in fierce competition for faculty members and students, considerations of academic survival must sometimes over-ride all objective budgetary yardsticks. Administrators must still be able to make *ad hoc* budgetary arrangements when this is necessary in order to recruit or retain faculty. And, especially in the "hard sciences," individual departments

[10] Aaron Wildavsky, in *The Politics of the Budgetary Process* (Boston: Little, Brown, 1964), p. 17, makes a helpful distinction between "the base" and the idea of "fair shares" or equity: "The base is the general expectation among the participants that programs will be carried on at close to the going level of expenditures but it does not necessarily include all activities. Having a project included in the agency's base thus means more than just getting it in the budget for a particular year. It means establishing the expectation that the expenditure will continue. . . . 'Fair share' means not only the base an agency has established but also the expectation that it will receive some proportion of funds, if any, which are to be increased over or decreased below the base of various governmental agencies. 'Fair share,' then, reflects a convergence of expectations on roughly how much the agency is to receive in comparison to others."

and even professors are able to obtain so much outside support for their activities that they can almost consider themselves independent of the university budget. In cases of this kind, if an administrator tried to impose firm budgetary controls over their funds, the professors might—and in some cases do—pull up their projects and their funds and go to another university. The academic market place today is simply not hospitable to administrators taking a "hard line" on budgetary decisions.

In short, modern budgeting has not eliminated horseback judgement, or the play of environmental pressures, from budgetary decisions. Nor can it be said that scientific budgeting has greatly lightened the burdens of the administrator. The tasks of data gathering and paperwork have increased voluminously in practically every institution where modern budgetary procedures have been introduced. This has caused no small amount of concern among faculty members as well as the administrators who are faced with the mounting necessity of filling out budget reports. Finally, it should be restated that while modern budgeting has shifted the locale of conflict over budgetary decisions and in some cases reduced tension in this area, it has by no means ushered in an era of good feeling in the allocation of resources in higher education.

Yet despite the restraints imposed upon modern budgeting by problems of measurement and the character of academic life, the techniques of modern budgeting are very much in evidence. Herein lies one of the intriguing anomalies of scientific management in higher education. Reforms in university budgeting, at least as far as university officials are able to describe the motives inspiring management innovation, have been less a response to the inner necessities of university management than they have been a response to legal requirements or strategic calculations in dealing with the external world, most notably the state legislature and state co-ordinating boards. It is to an examination of these outside pressures that we now turn.

THE TWO FACES OF ACADEMIC BUDGETING

One common theme runs through a majority of the explanations which university officials give for their recent budgetary reforms: either an outside state agency required the change, or else the university decided that it should alter its procedures in order to compete more effectively with other institutions in the quest for public funds. In Florida and Virginia, for example, state co-ordinating boards have been most influential in suggesting or requiring reforms in budgeting procedures. In Missouri and Montana state budget offices have generated changes, while in Washington a new legislative budgeting and accounting act began a series of major budgetary revisions in higher education in the state.[11]

Formula Budgeting

The use of formulas in particular has been heavily shaped by external considerations. In one major university which was under no formal obligation to use these yardsticks a vice-president explained the university's use of formulas in preparing and submitting a budget request in these words: "We use the displays that give us the best image." Others have expressed the motive less candidly but the sentiments are similar. Some officials stated that they felt compelled to adopt formulas when competing institutions began to use them, fearing that they would be at a disadvantage in the legislature if they failed to go along with the new techniques. Others felt that formulas would aid academic administrators in their lobbying activity in the state legislature.

Young institutions sometimes have a special interest in the use of formulas for budget requests. They want to catch up with the established institutions, or at least to protect themselves against well-entrenched universities which tend to regard new institutions with suspicion. A budgeting system geared to cost or enrollment formulas provides the necessary appropriations for young institutions to grow to a point of self-sufficiency.

Leading universities, on the other hand, may easily be placed in jeopardy by the adoption of standardized techniques for allocating funds among institutions. More often than not, the principal university has higher per capita costs as a result of its expensive research and graduate programs as well as higher salary scales designed to hold distinguished professors. In states that use a student-faculty ratio as a basis for allocating funds to individual institutions, it is virtually a matter of life and death to the large research universities to make certain that the special needs of high-cost programs are recognized in any formulas that are developed. By and large these universities have been able to achieve this goal, but each threatened change in the budget formula is a source of serious anxiety for the administrators of large universities.

One recurrent problem centers on the definition of a full-time-equivalent student. For undergraduate students in Texas, an FTE student is one who carries a fifteen-hour load. But to apply the same ratio to graduate programs at the University of Texas would virtually wreck the university. Consequently the state of Texas developed a new formula specifying that

[11] For further commentary on the relationship between state government and higher education in budgeting, see Moos and Rourke, *The Campus and the State*, Chapter 4.

twelve hours would give full-time-equivalent status to a master's student and nine hours to a Ph.D. candidate. Any shift in these ratios will produce reverberations throughout the system of higher education in Texas.

Thus the path of formula budgeting is full of perils, especially for major universities, but the opportunities for dramatic improvements in appropriations are also present. And while university administrators remain somewhat ambivalent toward the use of formulas, most academic officials from any type of institution would be inclined to agree with the university budget officer who told us in an interview that formulas serve three essential functions in academic budgeting:

1. "They reduce tension, bickering, and throat cutting among the institutions."
2. "They have protected our appropriations base, and since our formula is geared to enrollments, we have some guarantees of continued increases as long as the formula is used."
3. "The research university can still insist on appropriations larger than the formula allows."

University and co-ordinating board administrators are not the only public officials with an interest in budgeting formulas. Legislative officials, too, have been quick to see the advantage of using formulas in appropriating funds for higher education. Many legislators assert that the determination of an over-all level of support for higher education within a state—a lump sum figure for the total higher education budget—can be made rather quickly in any legislative session. The real conflict arises over the distribution of funds among state institutions of higher education. It is here that an allocation formula enters the picture as a politically acceptable means of slicing the academic pie. A budgetary formula gives a legislator three things he very much desires: simplification, political protection, and a means of reducing conflict with his colleagues.

First of all, a legislator must find a way of reducing the complex issues of higher educational finance to manageable dimensions. Formulas are a convenient way of doing this. A student-teacher ratio provides a handy rule-of-thumb for deciding on faculty size at any institution. So do formulas for levels of library support or nonacademic staffing. Even when they rest on shaky empirical foundations, budget formulas make it vastly easier for the legislator to see the full picture of higher education, although the picture may be carefully tinted by individual institutions to prevent a legislature from jumping to damaging conclusions about their operations.[12]

Secondly, budgeting formulas provide a legislator with a certain amount of political protection from his constituents. By accepting a standard

[12] For an analysis of the process of simplification in budgeting in the national government, see Wildavsky, *The Politics of the Budgetary Process*, pp. 11–12.

formula as a basis for appropriations to higher education, legislators find it somewhat easier to explain the steady increases in costs that have taken place in this area since World War II. This is especially valuable for legislators in districts without local universities. These legislators may appreciate the necessity for continued support of academic institutions, but they are under heavy pressures to support noneducational projects of one kind or another in their own districts.

Thirdly, budget formulas, when they are carefully employed, may tend to reduce conflict among legislators over the allocation of funds to individual institutions. Formulas have not banished bargaining and the exchange of special favors. Nor have legislators always hewed exactly to the line determined by formula calculations. But formulas used on a statewide basis force the institutions to come to some rough agreement among themselves before the issues are carried to the legislature. And they give the legislator a starting place in his negotiations with other legislators.

The fact that formulas are essentially rules-of-thumb designed to stabilize relationships within the educational system needs to be underscored. These formulas are not designed to produce precise calibrations of educational needs. Certainly they do not rest to any appreciable extent upon research that links the formula in question to the effectiveness of the educational process. Again, the problem of measurement is involved. No one has yet devised a plausible way of proving that a 15-to-1 student-teacher ratio gives the greatest education for the least cost. To the extent that formulas have any empirical base at all, they are most likely to rest on a ratio or cost which simply happened to be in existence at the time the formula was devised. This ratio, virtually an accident of history, then becomes a point of departure for future calculations of needs. From time to time the formula will be modified as a result of new studies or under pressure from growing institutions, but the original formula stands a good chance of retaining its essential character for a number of years.

Regardless of how a formula is calculated, however, it is not used extensively for management inside the campus. For a good many years the University of Minnesota used rough formulas as a means of drawing up its legislative requests. Finally the administration also decided to use a formula as the basis for the actual division of new funds for faculty salaries within the institution. The outcry and backlash were so substantial that the administration abandoned internal formulas altogether but held on to the formula approach in dealing with the state legislature.

Cost Analysis

Like formulas, cost analysis also appears to be developed by universities and colleges primarily to deal with outside agencies rather than for interna management purposes. At Indiana University, for example, sophisticated cost analysis is carried out for instruction, costs of central services, physical plant maintenance, and a variety of other activities.[13] The studies began under a mandate from the state legislature requiring the four state institutions to reach agreement on a single request for operating funds based on an analysis of their operations. So far, however, the cost studies have been used primarily for the purpose of preparing the legislative budget rather than as a means of determining the allocation of funds within each institution.

Even in the external budget, cost analysis may not be integrally connected to the budget formulas. Cost analysis may provide interesting displays in the appendix of the budget, but formulas for future requests are commonly developed quite independently of costs. University financial officials have tended to keep cost analysis separate from the development of budget formulas because they serve quite distinct purposes in university administration. To bring them together opens the Pandora's box of possibilities: first, that the fate of internal programs will be decided purely on the basis of cost—which spells trouble for many necessary but high-cost programs; secondly, that legislatures might grant appropriations to universities which do their work most cheaply rather than most effectively; and thirdly, that higher education as a whole will be judged, by the public and by its critics, in terms of how low its costs are. Miraculously, these possibilities do not occur very often. But evidence that they occasionally do occur is enough to strike fear in the hearts of sensitive administrators, who feel that costs and quantification, at their present stage of development, are extremely poor indicators of university performance.[14]

It is not surprising, then, that cost analysis, which presumably records the past and present, is used by institutions less frequently than budget formulas, which project into the future. This is another way of saying that some colleges and universities have developed means of getting what they need for the future without knowing much about the costs of their current operations. In our survey, 53.3 per cent of the schools used both formulas and cost analysis; 25.3 per cent used formulas without any cost analysis to support the formulas; 15.5 per cent used neither. But only 5.9 per cent reported that they used cost analysis without making use of budget formulas. The practice of using quantification for predicting future needs when it is not considered reliable for the analysis of current operations

[13] For a detailed review of the Indiana procedures, see Lee Hull and D. A. McWhirter, *Unit Cost Analysis Procedure: Indiana University* (Bloomington: Bureau of Institutional Research, Indiana University, 1964).

[14] See Lee Hull, "Pitfalls in the Use of Unit Cost Studies," *Journal of Higher Education*, XXXII, No. 7 (October, 1961), 371–76.

may seem somewhat bizarre, but in the view of a number of university officials it is a logical and necessary strategy for institutional survival.

The Ladder of Objectivity

The pressures within a university from faculty and students militate in favor of subjective, personalized, individualized decision making in budgetary matters. The pressures outside the institution, from the legislature or the state co-ordinating board, militate in favor of rigorously quantified budgetary decisions. As a result, something resembling a ladder of objectivity has emerged in the budgeting process in higher education.[15] At the bottom of the ladder, within academic departments and in small university agencies, budgeting is still carried on in a highly subjective way. Primary consideration is still given to such factors as the pressures of the academic market place, and the idiosyncracies of individual faculty members. Further up the ladder, in the office of the dean, quantitative yardsticks are available, but the dean uses them with caution. As a means of convincing an irate chairman that he cannot add new staff members in the coming year, the dean may choose to show the chairman unit cost figures which prove that the department is already one of the most expensive on campus. But virtually every dean we interviewed was quick to point out that it was necessary to tolerate high-cost departments under certain conditions, as for example, when a department is heavily freighted with senior but not very distinguished men, and the only way to improve departmental standing, tenure being what it is, is to add still more staff.

Moving another rung up the ladder, in the offices of the financial vice-president, the provost, and the president, the subjectivity of the process on the lower levels collides with the quantifications demanded by the state legislature. Yet even at this level decisions are seldom made exclusively on the basis of quantitative formulas or straight cost analysis.

Finally, in state co-ordinating boards and in the committees of the state legislature, policy makers work with vast aggregates of figures, and the tendency to make decisions in terms of quantitative yardsticks becomes considerably more pronounced. At this level the personal problems of the individual professor or department count relatively little, while the student-teacher ratio may be of central importance.

In some instances, the cross pressure on the budgetary process is so intense that a college or university may actually resort to a double system of budgeting. One system follows a format and procedures satisfactory for

[15] Two perceptive observers of budgeting helped to clarify our thinking on this subject. They are Errol Mauchlan, Budget Officer of the Berkeley Campus of the University of California, and Lee Hull, Associate Director of Institutional Research at Indiana University.

the internal management of the institution. The other system—quite literally maintained as separate books—satisfies the demands from the outside. Where such dual systems exist the internal budget is more likely to be a program budget, while the external budget required by the state legislature is more likely to be of the old-fashioned object variety. This is true, for example, in the budgeting procedures of the University of Massachusetts, the State University of New York at Buffalo, and the University of North Dakota. These institutions have followed the essentials of the American Council on Education model for their internal operation but have developed separate object budgets to meet the requirements of their state governments.

Budgeting and Internal Control

In spite of the dominant emphasis on external factors in budgeting, it would be misleading to suggest that nothing has happened to the internal operation of institutions of higher education as a result of reforms in the budgetary process. On the contrary, two internal developments flowing from innovations in budgeting have had a great deal of importance. First, along with the emergence of new budgeting theories and procedures in higher education, colleges and universities have begun to establish specialized budget offices with responsibility for the preparation and control of the academic budget. In one-fourth of the state colleges and universities replying to our questionnaire, specialized budget offices are now in existence. In the remainder, budgeting responsibility is customarily lodged in the business office or the comptroller's office, without being identified specifically with a budget office.

In most of the cases where a specialized budget office has been established it is a subordinate agency of the business office, or, as is the case at Florida State University, of the comptroller's office. Elsewhere the budget officer reports to a vice-president for business and finance, as he does at the University of Washington, or in many instances directly to the president, as he does at Ohio State.

The development of specialized budget offices has certainly not been as rapid as the emergence of offices of institutional research or central computer facilities. In part, this may be explained by the fact that computer work and institutional research are relatively new activities, while budgeting has been a traditional responsibility of the universities and has long been carried on by the business officer or by the president himself. It is not surprising, therefore, that functional specialization in budgeting should emerge as a subordinate role within an established agency. In computer work, by contrast, data processing represented an entirely new departure for university administration and there was no existing office in which this new function could readily be located.[16]

A second change that reforms in the format and techniques of budgeting have brought is a shift in the locus of budgetary decisions. What seems to have happened in many universities is a simultaneous centralization of the *preparation* of the budget and a decentralization of the *administration* of the budget once the funds are appropriated or allocated. Thus in a modern university with a program budget, formulas, and cost analysis, the president and his top financial officials very often make the key decisions in preparing the general university budget for presentation to the state legislature. But once the money is made available, the president will usually delegate control over the expenditure of these appropriations to his deans, allowing them a maximum of flexibility and discretion in switching funds around as they find necessary.

The University of Washington is a well-developed example of these countervailing movements in budgeting. Under the administration of President Odegaard the university established a highly detailed, rigorously controlled program budget. Each department and college was required to submit detailed information on all phases of budget requests. This information was put on standard forms which were established by the central administration in accordance with programs determined by the president. This gave the chief executive as much information about university activities as his subordinates possessed, and in some cases decidedly more data. In a hierarchical organization this would be taken for granted, perhaps, but in a university with a highly diffuse distribution of power the president may be almost totally dependent on information supplied him by the deans. Before the new budget system was introduced at the University of Washington, there appears to have been just such a decentralization of authority, with loosely confederated colleges making the effective determinations on their own budget requests while the central administration did little more than ratify these requests. With new program budgeting procedures, the university now has powerful means of shaping its budget centrally.

But once the legislature has appropriated money, the University of Washington farms these funds out to the deans for the details of expenditure. Thus several deans, at the University of Washington and elsewhere,

[16] The presence of a specialized budget office also appears to be a clear function of the size of the institution. Only 11.7 per cent of the schools responding to our questionnaire with fewer than 2,000 students had budget offices. 17.8 per cent of those with between 2,000 and 10,000 students had a specialized budget office, and 48.8 per cent of those over 10,000 indicated the existence of such an office. See Appendix B, p. 145, Table B-14.

told us that a conversion to centralized budgeting had deprived them of discretion in budget preparation but had, if anything, enhanced their freedom to make expenditure decisions. A number of universities, among them Purdue, Ohio State, and the University of California, reported similar decentralization of expenditure controls as a part of their program of budget reform.

Along with budget reforms, however, has come an enlarged role for financial officers. Even though there is some indication that expenditures are being controlled at lower levels—or at least that lower levels have not given up all influence over expenditure—the chief financial officer, under the direction of the president, has enhanced his potential control over all phases of resource allocation as a result of the new modes of budgeting. This control may not appear immediately. But in a period when funds suddenly become extremely scarce, the new power of budget officials will be unmistakable.

At one large university we studied, academic officials—the deans, the provost, and the academic vice-president—had been strong supporters of budget reform during a period of great expansion and relative affluence of the university. Eventually the university had established new standard procedures in budget reporting and preparation. Control over these procedures was lodged in the central budget office. Up to this point in the reform movement there were few complications. But when student enrollments dramatically exceeded expectations, the university's budget was suddenly strained. A conflict developed between the financial hierarchy, which now controlled decisions in areas involving the availability of funds, and the academic hierarchy, which felt that it should continue to make decisions concerning the academic program. Financial officials argued that they, and they alone, knew "how much the university could afford," and academic administrators had no effective way of answering this contention. Their only recourse was to demand the creation of a budget council consisting of both academic and financial officials, which would have ultimate power to make fiscal decisions having critical program effects.

Shifts in the effective power of decision in budgeting, then, do not occur all at once. Nor do they become final. Periods of growth and affluence appear more likely to leave decision-making power in the hands of academic officials and to invite widespread decentralization of expenditure. Periods of serious scarcity, which may be episodic or may extend over a long period of time, tend to give more power to financial officials and to push a university toward centralized decision making in the expenditure of funds as well as in the preparation of the budget.

NEW DIRECTIONS IN BUDGETING

Up to now colleges and universities have done little more than introduce into their own operations budgetary techniques and programs developed as early as the 1930's in business and government. A few universities, however, have begun to look beyond the boundaries of program budgeting itself. In the University of California system, budget officials, in co-operation with the computer center, have been developing a complete budgetary model of the university system which will eventually be programed on the computer. A complete input-output system (as discussed in Chapter 2) will be displayed for university administrators. Such variables as cost, enrollment, and staffing, as well as other important factors included in the model, can then be manipulated to study what effects changes in one area might have on the total university budget. So far, few universities have followed this lead, although some are giving it careful study.

In North Carolina, again largely under pressure from state agencies, the public colleges and universities have developed a system known as "alternative budgeting."[17] Under this procedure academic institutions actually develop two different budget requests, labeled an "A" budget and a "B" budget. The "A" request indicates the activities that will be carried on if the institution continues to operate at approximately its present level of financial support. The "B" budget spells out, in a manner coming close to the hopes of real performance budgeting, what the institution will be able to do with increased funds. This is, of course, in line with the traditional legislative practice of focusing attention on new items in the budget, rather than on requests for continued support of existing programs. The alternative budget is a highly systematic means of highlighting changes between present and future levels of support.

Perhaps more important for the immediate future is the concept of statewide budgeting for institutions of higher education being developed by many co-ordinating boards. Except for a few states, such as South Dakota, Oregon, and Georgia, the idea of statewide budgeting is new for higher education. But once the co-ordinating boards succeed in establishing comparable budget categories for each institution and develop cost analysis techniques which permit easy interinstitutional comparisons, there is an increasing possibility that the same sort of upward shift of power which has occurred within many institutions will occur for the entire state system. That is to say that when co-ordinating boards are properly instrumented—and some of them already are—there are strong indications that

[17] For a detailed description of this process in government, see Lewis, "Toward a Theory of Budgeting."

they will centralize power in budget preparation, leaving budget administration in the hands of the individual institutions. But once a central co-ordinating board has demonstrated its capacity to supervise the preparation of a statewide budget, it will be in a strong position to exercise detailed control over expenditures as well. Certainly this sequence of controls has occurred within individual institutions. But we reserve judgment as to whether this will also happen within a state system. The political position and the administrative capacity of most co-ordinating board staffs is not the same as that of a university office of finance. And in most states there would be deeply rooted opposition to the establishment of a totally integrated system of higher education.

In any case the outcome here depends upon a variety of factors outside the control of academic officials. A depression in the American economy could have a profound effect on budgeting procedures as well as on allocations within the educational budget. More stringent methods of allocating funds—a virtual rationing program—could even become part of the picture. With the groundwork for budgetary control established during a period of expanding expenditures, university administrations have now equipped themselves with formidable instruments of financial management for lean years if they should develop. Some of these same considerations apply to another area of resource allocation—the management of space.

THE EMERGING ROLE OF SPACE MANAGEMENT

Space management is easily one of the most highly rationalized areas of university administration. As one college official commented to us, "If science has really entered the halls of academe, it is in this field." About one-half of all state universities with more than 2,000 students have a Co-ordinator of Space or some similar officer, who is generally charged with compiling information about the use of space on campus, allocating the area presently available, and participating in the planning of capital construction projects. Much of this work is dependent upon standardization and the development of quantitative yardsticks. In the course of time the standards set and the decisions made by those controlling space have significant effects on the internal power structure of a university, on budgeting, on outside political support, and, indirectly at least, on the academic program itself.

The impetus for improving space management has come from two major sources. Since World War II the upsurge of enrollments on university campuses has led many administrators to institute space inventories and utilization studies in order to tackle short-run overcrowding and scheduling problems. At the same time, legislators, building authorities, state boards of higher education, and budget officers have begun to insist upon more adequate justification for additional capital construction than enrollment figures and presidential blandishments alone. Such outside pressure has been passed on by top university administrators to the schools and departments within their own institutions whose demands generate the need for more space. When the Indiana legislature instructed its state schools to develop general budgeting formulas, it also required the schools to prepare similar formulas for capital planning and construction.[18] In Florida the State Board of Control of Higher Education staff sees space utilization analysis as a potential tool to rationalize capital budget requests and has, therefore, conducted studies leading to the adoption of uniform standards for determining building needs in the state university system.

These twin pressures toward more efficient utilization of space—enrollment pressure from below and legislative budgetary pressure from above—have been felt in different ways by individual institutions. Both size and region appear to play a significant role in determining whether a specialized office of space utilization or planning is established on campus. Larger schools are significantly more likely to have such an office than smaller institutions. Among schools with an enrollment over 10,000, 74 per cent have a space office, as opposed to only 12 per cent of schools with fewer than 2,000 students. Surprisingly, there are also wide regional variations in the development of space utilization offices. In the South only 19 per cent of all schools have created space offices, while in the West more than 65 per cent have done so. This regional variation is partly explained by the concentration in the South of small schools, which are unlikely to bother with formal rationalization of the space use (43 per cent of all schools with less than 2,000 enrollment are in the South). But another and more significant factor is certainly the dramatic upswing in enrollment experienced by western schools, which in turn has generated larger and larger legislative appropriations for higher education and a corresponding growth of state interest in the efficiency and economy with which resources are being used. Since the West has felt these pressures most acutely, it is logical that this region should be in the vanguard of space management innovation.

There is some evidence also that western space administrators have, initially from necessity and later from conviction, been among the first to identify themselves as professional or semi-professional space management specialists. Once such a process has begun as a response to the pressures already noted, a pattern of cross-fertilization may take place

[18] James F. Blakesley, W. Charles Sherwood, and Fred E. Williams, "Capital Requirements Study," presented at the Workshop Seminar on Planning Physical Facilities for Higher Education, University of Wisconsin, June 16, 1964, p. 1.

within the region, accelerating the introduction, first, of highly rationalized space utilization techniques and, later, of specialized space offices. This suggests a certain insularity within regions, depending upon the existence of fairly subtle but unmistakable barriers against administrative mobility from one region to another.

The Administration of Space

Administrators in all regions would be quick to agree that one of the principal factors responsible for bringing space management to such an advanced state of rationalization is simply the fact that space is so easy to quantify. Square feet and student stations are quite measurable items, as are the hours and classifications ordinarily used in space studies. Simple scheduling processes and property records contain the rudimentary data necessary for this kind of quantification. If demands for efficiency and the pressures of external constituencies have increased the pace of rationalization in space management, this process has also been accelerated by the comparative ease of measuring space and its various uses.

There are four fairly distinct phases to university space management. The first is space inventory. Listings of all instructional space and, generally at a later time, of all campus space are compiled, and the space is classified according to rather rigid categories of use. This task has been appreciably facilitated by the use of electronic data-processing equipment. Secondly, space utilization studies are carried out. These studies attempt to determine the number of hours rooms are used per week and the number of student stations filled when the rooms are in use. The studies also may determine unit costs of operation. The data thus obtained, usually in terms of averages for whole categories of space (typical categories are listed in Table 4–3), are then set against standards of efficient space utilization, derived as a rule from the practice of other institutions.[19] It is then decided whether more use should be made of existing space or whether the amount of space in certain categories should actually be reduced. Initially both space inventories and utilization studies require standardized reporting of information from schools and departments. Both provide the background for the remaining two facets of space management, the allocation of existing space and capital planning.

The task of allocating space may or may not be carried out by the same administrative unit which conducts inventories and utilization studies. A major purpose at this point is to achieve a more efficient use of space. More than that, however, the notion that space should be distributed

[19] Very commonly used as a source of such standards is John Dale Russell and James I. Doi, *Manual for Space Utilization in Colleges and Universities* (Athens, Ohio: American Association of Collegiate Registrars and Admissions Officers, 1957).

TABLE 4–3: AREAS OF SPACE PROGRAM SUBJECT TO COST ANALYSIS

Area	No. of Schools	% (n = 266)
Cost of student residence space	119	45
Maintenance cost	108	41
Cost of classroom space	84	32
Cost of office space	64	24
Development and planning	50	19

equitably also comes into play, reflecting an acculturated assumption rather than any specific pressures. It is simply assumed that each department ought to be treated alike with respect to office and classroom space, except for differences that arise out of the instructional program itself. In any event, the pattern followed is a standard one. Each department is allotted a certain amount of office and research space according to a set formula; it may also be allotted classroom and laboratory space, but the tendency is for these facilities to be parceled out by a central scheduling unit as they are needed.

Space management also involves the estimation of future space needs for capital-planning programs, and the allocation of space in new buildings to various departments and agencies. Only rarely does the office responsible for space allocation also have jurisdiction over capital planning, but space allocation techniques nonetheless play an important role here. As Table 4–4 indicates, over 40 per cent of the state schools responding to our questionnaire use some sort of formula in campus planning.

TABLE 4–4: QUANTITATIVE FORMULAS USED IN SPACE MANAGEMENT

Purpose	No. of Schools	% (n = 266)
Determining classroom size	120	45
Long-range planning of building needs	116	43
Determining faculty office size	109	41
Determining size of student residences	90	34
Assignment of classroom space	80	30
Assignment of faculty offices	65	24
Assignment of students to residences	46	17
Renovation	1	—
Determining facilities to be razed	1	—
Planning student recreational areas	1	—

It should be noted, of course, that there are sharp upper limits on the value of space utilization studies in making decisions on the planning and development of a campus building program. These studies or the formulas to which they give rise are highly useful in allocating space within buildings once they are constructed or in determining the size of buildings before they are put up, but such studies cannot automatically generate decisions on the order in which buildings are to be constructed. They do not, for example, eliminate uncertainty as to whether higher priority should be given to a new science facility or to a classroom building. Top-level decisions of this kind must still be made in terms of some rather imprecise judgment of relative need, or, as is often the case, in terms of the relative pressure which rival claimants for additional space can exert. Moreover, in the ordinary practice of universities, any opportunity that opens up to obtain funds for the construction of a building far down on the priority list must be seized before it is lost. Priorities thus tend to be colored by expediency—a not altogether irrational policy, given the varied needs which most institutions of higher education have had with respect to capital construction during the recent period of expansion.

Once questions of priorities have been settled, the space manager resumes an active role in planning. Here has evolved one of the more interesting relationships between space management and academic programing. Many institutions have taken the approach that a department's present academic program, together with projected changes in enrollment and staff size, provide a sufficient indication of the department's future facility needs. It is assumed that class size, course offerings, laboratory requirements, and the like will remain roughly the same. However, some space managers have been concerned about the fact that steps once taken in physical development may limit future instructional innovation. Moreover, they believe that physical planning offers an opportunity for thorough re-evaluation of existing techniques of instruction.[20] Consequently these planners are beginning to ask the departments to look ahead, and they hold out the promise of appropriate facilities for a department which intends to revise its instructional approach.

One planning officer said that he and his staff became aware of this relationship between planning and academic programs only after they had made a number of decisions about the allocation of space in proposed buildings. They promptly moved to let the departments specify how they

[20] See especially Thomas R. Mason, "*Rural Italian*" *Goes Space Age* (Boulder: Office of Institutional Research and Planning, University of Colorado, mimeo., 1964), and John X. Jamrich, "Planning College Facilities," in Edwin F. Hallenbeck and Leo F. Redfern (eds.), *A College Colloquim on Institutional Research* (Kingston: Office of Institutional Research, University of Rhode Island, 1962).

envisioned their future academic programs, in order that administrative decisions would not force those programs into an inappropriate mold.

This serves to point up the fact that planning is an area of space allocation in which departments and faculties can play a significant role. While it is seldom true that faculty members are directly consulted about space utilization standards or even the existing allocation of classrooms and other space, departments and faculty committees generally are involved in capital planning. It is at this point that space allocation in projected buildings may become a matter of hard bargaining between faculty members and space allocators. Departmental estimates of future enrollments, for example, may not agree with those of the administration, even though the administration, with its research facilities, is likely to have the more detailed analysis on its side. The department may also be impressed with certain "needs" on the basis of tradition or examples set by other universities, "needs" which can be challenged by space managers. For example, one midwestern space director insists that departments always tend to ask for large auditoriums or lecture halls, even when they do not actually offer large lecture courses.

In the end, this process involves bargaining and compromise to settle disputes. The granting of office space to departments in lump sums, a very common practice, is one way in which conflict can be reduced. Another method of meeting conflict is exemplified by the University of Illinois, which defines five kinds of instructional space—classrooms, teaching laboratories, research area, faculty offices, and libraries—for the purposes of space allocation. Classrooms, libraries, and, to some extent, teaching laboratories are said to be related not to the departmental programs but to the enrollment of the university, thus removing them somewhat from the relevant area of bargaining. The availability of federal funds for certain research purposes, however, may give departments strong leverage against centrally controlled space allotments in this bargaining process.

There is one very general relationship between space management and academic programing which deserves comment. Consider for a moment the effects of the distribution of classes over the hours of the day and the days of the week. If all classes at an institution were held at the same time, there would have to be as many rooms as there are individual classes. On the other hand, if every class met at a different time, only one classroom would be needed. Obviously neither alternative is practical, but it can be seen that more efficient utilization of space should result from expanded, more even distribution of classes over the course of a week. In any event, space utilization studies seem to be followed, almost universally, by pressures for longer academic weeks, greater use of afternoon and evening time, and more classes on Tuesdays, Thursdays, and Saturdays. Improved utilization of space has even been used as a prime argument for adoption of the tri-mester system in a number of institutions.[21]

The academic effects of this "more efficient" use of space have been subject to considerable debate. Officials at Purdue, which is far advanced in central scheduling practices, maintain that the individual student is given greater choice among courses through an extended schedule than he receives on a schedule which provides for a large percentage of classes that meet at the same peak hours. Opponents of the new science of space management contend that students as well as professors may be better off if they can cluster their classes in the mornings, leaving afternoons and evenings free for extended study or research projects.

One outcome of the scarcity of space is the increased control of course scheduling by central space managers. At Purdue and Minnesota, for instance, space management and scheduling are functions of the same office. Traditional methods of scheduling, under which departments are asked what courses they wish to offer and at what times, are slowly giving way to the central allotment of time.[22] It is also becoming increasingly apparent that more efficient scheduling requires not only a central authority for the scheduling of classes but also some central control over the assignment of students to particular sections. This has been accomplished at the University of Massachusetts and at Purdue University by means of a computer scheduling system which does not ordinarily give students the option of selecting among particular course sections. Other universities, including Illinois, Indiana, and Minnesota, are moving in the same general direction.

Internal Competition for Space

The allocation of space, like budgeting, is a matter of distributing scarce or limited resources. It involves decisions about programs and priorities. Consequently changes in the process of space allocation bring shifts in the relative positions of power and wealth of various segments of the university community. Unless these rationalizing devices of space management are simply window dressing (and, indeed, even if they are), they will alter the institution's power structure, bringing gains and losses for various groups within the university.

The most obvious changes brought about by the intrusion of rationalized space management is a shift of some kinds of traditional authority

[21] See Technical Committee on Institutional Capacities and Area Needs, *Institutional Capacities and Area Needs of California Public Higher Education, 1960–1975* (Berkeley: Office of the President, University of California, 1961), p. 26 and *The Utilization of Instructional Space in the State University System of Florida: Fall 1962* (Tallahassee: Board of Control of Higher Education, 1962), pp. 56–58.

[22] Technical Committee on Institutional Capacities and Area Needs, *Institutional Capacities and Area Needs of California Public Higher Education, 1960–1975*, p. 25.

and prerogatives from faculty departments and colleges to central administrators. For example, many university space managers have indicated that a traditional pattern, that of granting departments buildings which are then placed under departmental control, has been giving way steadily to the demands for more efficient utilization of facilities and standardized allotments of space for offices and research and classroom space. Moreover, as indicated above, the traditional faculty prerogative of setting the time at which classes meet is being reduced by administrators seeking more efficient scheduling.

At a number of institutions there is an increasing tendency for space administrators to question faculty control over class size. A recent space utilization report at the University of Rhode Island, for example, went so far as to say that "rooms should be scheduled according to student station capacity, rather than section size limitations requested by departments, subject to particular educational requirements for some sections."[23] This statement is a very clear call for a shift in authority in the area of space management.

It is somewhat more difficult to determine if a similar shift of influence has occurred at the planning stage. Faculty committees are commonly included in any planning procedure, and, as mentioned earlier, faculty members are consulted about their future academic plans by a number of administrative planners. Nevertheless, space managers have a large part in determining how much space is to be given a department moving to a new building, as well as how that space is to be divided among various categories of use.[24]

This is not to say that the space management practices discussed here invariably lead to pitched battles between professors and administrators. There are a number of reasons, of course, why this does not happen. First of all, space administrators have not been unaware of the academic implications of their policies. A common theme among them is that the more efficient use of space frees funds for faculty salaries which might otherwise have to be devoted to capital construction.[25] In addition, there is a good deal of reassurance from space managers that utilization is not an end in itself. One Big Ten space official simply puts it this way: "Some inefficiency is the price of a great institution." Another official somewhat wryly com-

[23] *Study of Space Utilization for the Fall Semester, 1963* (Kingston: Office of Institutional Research and Planning, University of Rhode Island, 1964), p. 6.

[24] For a pertinent listing of some "factors inhibiting the improvement of space use," see John X. Jamrich, "Studying Utilization of Instructional Facilities in Colleges and Universities," in Hallenbeck and Redfern (eds.), *A College Colloquium*, pp. 38–40. These factors reflect traditional areas of faculty or decentralized authority.

[25] *Ibid.*, p. 31.

mented, "The most inefficient use of space we have on campus is the football stadium, and certainly no one is proposing to change that."

Indeed, faculties do not always fare badly in the change to new modes of space management. At some institutions, such as the University of Minnesota and the University of California at Berkeley, faculty committees have strong influence in determining space standards and in planning. Other faculties, such as those at the University of Washington and Purdue, have indeed been rewarded with substantial salary increases accompanying more rationalized management techniques. Finally, as Wildavsky has said in another context, ". . . the disinclination of participants to utilize their political resources to the fullest extent undoubtedly leaves broad areas of inertia and inattention open for change. Thus the 'slack' in the system may leave considerable room for ingenuity and innovation. . . ."[26] This "slack" certainly exists in various degrees in all university communities.

One area which illustrates the accommodation emerging between faculty members and space managers is the allocation of office space. It is reported both from the University of Minnesota and the University of California that faculty members demanded more individual office space than the 120 square feet that space allocators were willing to grant but were careful not to demand a figure so large that double occupancy would be encouraged. They settled on compromise figures of 135 and 140 square feet, figures which are in no sense empirically justified but were, rather, the outcome of practical bargaining.

In more general ways, the application of rationalized space management methods can lead to a redistribution of resources. One example can be seen at the University of California, where utilization studies indicated that present practices were far short of meeting modern standards of efficient use. The university held up its building program until utilization could be improved. On a number of campuses space management has led to a shift of emphasis from the expansion of classroom capacity to the development of other facilities, such as research areas and office space. The long-standing assumption that universities lacked classroom facilities gave way in the face of contradictory evidence to programs designed to increase the utilization of existing classroom space. For example, enrollment at the University of Illinois grew 37 per cent in the few years after the establishment of a space office, but the number of classrooms in use actually decreased by two. At the same time, much greater emphasis was placed upon the development of office, research, and laboratory facilities.

[26] Wildavsky, *The Politics of the Budgetary Process*, p. 143.

Pressures from Outside

To an important extent the development of rationalized techniques of space management has its roots in the external relations of the university. As noted earlier, legislatures and state boards of higher education, along with state budget offices, have often demanded the use of rational techniques in handling space problems. And many institutions have considered that it is to their advantage in competing for financial and political support to introduce these new management practices. Moreover, a number of institutions within a state may themselves adopt formulas and standards in order to prevent strident public competition for funds and the imposition by the legislature of a statewide board of control. This has been the case in Colorado, for example.

The selection and display of data regarding space utilization may assume strategic importance in the context of an institution's external relations. An example from the current scene points up the issues involved. The space director at one midwestern university has been very concerned about cost data compiled by the Board of Higher Education which compares utilization at the university with that of other state institutions. On the surface the university appears to compare unfavorably with other schools, and it is, therefore, attempting to press for additional staff on the State Board, so that proper attention can be given in future space studies to the special characteristics of university programs which require higher levels of space utilization.

Particularly sensitive issues are raised by the use of space formulas in planning new buildings. These formulas are generally expressed in terms of square feet per student or staff member for various classifications of space. Very often they are derived from "a picture taken at a moment of time" at a single institution or of several institutions involved in a comparative study. The University of Minnesota, for example, found that it had one senior faculty member for every three enrolled graduate students. This ratio was used without further study to plan future space allotments for senior faculty members.

It is in fact very difficult to place space formulas on a solid empirical footing. At one midwestern university a graduate thesis designed to explore the effects of classroom environments upon learning found that classroom size or shape had no significant effects on the learning that occurred in the class. Because the thesis did not provide a rationale for space allocation and, in fact, de-emphasized the importance of space altogether, it has been largely ignored by the university's space managers. Purdue University has undertaken some experimental work with various sizes of offices for faculty and staff, and it is claimed that the Purdue standards for office space are optimal at least in terms of architectural standards, such as the placing of windows and doors.

A significant aspect of such standards, representing as they do averages and estimates, is that they can be subject to instant alteration whenever necessary. In one midwestern state where the colleges and universities submit a joint budget request to the legislature, these standards are often adjusted by interinstitutional agreement in order to achieve a desired level of appropriations.

Similarly, data in the hands of legislators or the board of higher education can be used flexibly to achieve specific purposes. In Florida, for example, the discovery that only 18 per cent of nonresidential space in the state university system is classified as "teaching facility" space has been cited by the State Board of Control as a reason for converting more campus space to instructional purposes and for holding back a capital construction program.[27] In the multi-campus University of California system the quantification of information and the development of standards dealing with space have generated considerable pressure for equality of treatment for every campus.

Space managers and administrators at individual institutions have been increasingly eager to urge upon governing boards, budget officers, legislators, and the general public the qualifications which must be kept in mind in interpreting statistical statements about space utilization and needs. One of the most common qualifications mentioned is the special needs generated by certain kinds of instructional programs. A technically oriented institution such as Purdue, for example, has a number of expensive and space-consuming programs which pull down raw averages of space utilization and space needs and raise unit costs per student. Of course, any state institution may find it necessary to carry on a high-cost, space-consuming program which attracts few students, such as the aeronautical engineering program at the University of Illinois. (It is, however, entirely possible that space utilization studies will eventually create greater interest in regional facilities for programs which do show a very low rate of utilization within a single state.)

A research-oriented university also faces difficulties. It may require large amounts of space, much of it of an expensive variety, and thus show poor utilization and high costs in comparative studies. Standards for research space are developing at a much slower pace than requirements for the use and allocation of instructional and office space. A university may also find itself in a disadvantageous position if its enrollment is stable

[27] *The Utilization of Instructional Space in the State University System of Florida*, pp. 60, 70.

even while its program is expanding. In this situation it becomes markedly more difficult to justify adding new buildings, and the university may face instead pressure for more efficient space management in existing facilities.

On the more positive side, institutions have found that the publication and display of data and statistics arising out of space studies can be effective instruments of public relations. Most institutions find that legislators and others are much more impressed with the value of development plans when they are presented in terms of space-need criteria, projected enrollment, rationalized cost analyses, or four-color diagrams showing the proposed development. In other words, the appearance of analytic, well-informed handling of planning is an asset to an institution in its efforts to achieve its physical development objectives.

BUDGETING AND SPACE MANAGEMENT: CONTRASTS AND COMPARISONS

The similarities between budgeting and space management procedures are striking but deceptive. Both have been subjected to considerably greater quantification and rationalization in recent years. Both use formulas, cost analysis, and computers. Both areas have begun to develop similar techniques for reporting and control of resources. And both areas have emerged as professional specialties as the space expert and the budget officer move into positions of growing responsibility in higher education.

In spite of these similarities, however, most universities treat budgeting and space management as two quite distinct activities. While the president of a university is ultimately responsible for both activities, and while these operations employ many common procedures, very little effort has been made to bring budgeting and space management under a single administrative roof. Under the direction of the president, financial officials carry on the day-to-day administration of the budget. Physical space, on the other hand, tends to be controlled rather firmly by other administrators. Only rarely does the chief business officer of a college or university have direct responsibility for space management.

Such a dual system of administration, with one set of officials responsible for budgeting and another group responsible for space management, has a definite rationale in administrative theory. "The advantage of such an arrangement," noted an American Council on Education Committee, "is that the financial officer, being thus relieved of the responsibility for operations, is able to take a more objective view of the physical plant and of the auxiliary activities than would be possible if they were under his direction."[28] But the preference of the American Council committee was for a system in which full control of the physical plant, including "campus development and building planning; space utilization; operation and maintenance of buildings and grounds; and related services . . ."[29] should be in the hands of the chief business officer of an educational institution.

Thus while the American Council recommendations on budgeting procedure have been widely accepted by institutions of higher education, the council's corresponding proposal to give financial officers full control of space management has largely been ignored. Although some universities assign space management responsibilities to their financial offices, these institutions are in a distinct minority. Of 168 institutions with no specialized space office, only 10 (about 6 per cent) give such responsibility to the business office.

When financial offices do exercise some powers of space management, they often share those powers with other university offices. At the University of Washington, for example, the business office controls space inventories, the registrar assigns classroom space, and the planning officer, who reports to the vice-president for academic affairs, is concerned with long-range problems in the physical plant. In space management there may be no single place at which all space problems are drawn together. Only rarely, in other words, does a university possess a space management document which is the equivalent of the budget document. Such a rarity is found in the University of California system, which has developed a highly rationalized statewide set of norms for space utilization and planning.

In spite of similarities in the style of operation, then, it appears that budgeting and space management represent two distinct administrative subcultures. There seems to be virtually no spillover from one area to another in a single institution. It was, for example, our original assumption that any school which used quantitative formulas in budgeting would also tend to use such yardsticks in space utilization. But statistical tests revealed no such association. To put it simply, budgetary practices appear to have no significant influence on space practices in a given college or university, and space practices do not influence budgetary practices to any notable degree.[30] Budget officers at one institution may inspire budgetary innovations in sister institutions without engendering any desire for more efficient space management practices on their own campus. The two areas appear to have developed independently of one another.

[28] American Council on Education, National Committee on the Preparation of a Manual on College and University Business Administration, *College and University Business Administration*, I (Washington: American Council on Education, 1952), 6.

[29] *Ibid.*, II, 18.

[30] See Appendix B, p. 150.

Within both areas, however, the movement is toward more and more centralized, rationalized, and specialized analysis. The pace of change has been rapid in the last decade, but neither budgeting nor space management has remotely exploited the full range of possibilities that lie ahead with the advent of computers and total information systems. Only a few institutions have ventured into these more sophisticated areas. Yet as long as such high-level analysis enhances the ability of academic institutions to survive in their quest for funds and space, it would seem quite consistent with the pattern of the last decade to expect continuing innovations in the future with respect to both budgeting and space management.

Chapter Five

NEW STYLES OF UNIVERSITY MANAGEMENT

In previous chapters we have described the innovation of specific practices which seem to herald a "managerial revolution" in higher education. These practices have been accompanied by certain changes in the general style of university administration. It is to an examination of these changes that we now turn, recognizing at the same time that we are here dealing with aspects of university administration which elude quantification and measurement. Except where otherwise noted, we shall therefore be relying much more heavily on interview than on questionnaire data in this chapter.

Four areas of change stand out as being particularly significant in the emerging style of university administration. The first is the shift from secrecy to publicity in the general conduct of administrative and academic affairs—a shift which has greatly altered the relationship between institutions of higher education and their environment. The second is the development, sometimes institutionalized and sometimes highly informal, of a cabinet style of government in place of the presidential system of executive leadership that has traditionally characterized university administration. The third is the introduction of new forms of decision making which, if not entirely as rational as their advocates might suggest, are nonetheless considerably less subjective than the purely intuitive styles of the past. Fourth, and finally, the multi-campus network that has been created in many state systems of higher education has generated both novel administrative forms and new difficulties as the world of higher education seeks to adjust to the demands of the modern age.

While the onset of the managerial revolution has had a perceptible effect on all schools, the extent of its influence was quite varied at the institutions visited in this survey. Some universities, which have just recently emerged from a teacher-training or agricultural college background and are pushing hard for improved quality in the face of bigger enrollments, tend to look upon the new techniques of management with unrestrained enthusiasm. One university we visited had only several years ago been a normal school. Its enrollments were burgeoning and the quality of its academic program, by the assessment of its own faculty, was deficient in comparison to the major state university. At the same time, the administration radiated an image of self-confidence. Exercising a high degree of control over academic and nonacademic policies, it used a full arsenal of modern management techniques to make and justify its decisions.

Newly established institutions have been equally vigorous in the application of fresh managerial procedures. The University of South Florida, opened in 1960, is organized and equipped in ways which are considerably more in keeping with precepts of modern management than with the administrative tradition in higher education. A Division of Instructional Services makes fullest use of television, radio, and audio-visual aids and looks upon the library as simply another component in the general system of instructional aids. The Data Processing Division of the university employs computers and other modern equipment to grade examinations, process library materials, and run programs in almost every area of university administration. An Office of Personnel Services actively recruits administrative and professional staff for the university and maintains centralized records on all faculty members. Unhampered by traditional forms of organization, the university is in a position to experiment boldly with these new forms. No one in the administration has to mark time waiting for old machines to wear out before replacing them with advanced new equipment. In hiring personnel the university has been able to recruit young men trained in modern techniques without having to wait for older personnel to retire.

For new or radically changing institutions, however, the revolution in management may indeed be a mixed blessing. In a context in which faculty members are less privileged and in which they often feel oppressed beneath the weight of administrative authority, the innovations wrought by the new devices of management may deepen the sense of faculty alienation and intensify the antagonism, latent and overt, which has traditionally existed between the administrative and the academic cultures. In this respect the new modes of management may increase the capacity for administrative control only at the price of making it more difficult to attract and hold a faculty upon whose quality the institution's drive for intellectual advancement and academic status actually depends.

The University of South Florida, for example, with all its accoutrements of modern organization, equipment, and personnel, could not avoid a tangled political controversy that arose over the cancellation of a contract offered a professor of political science. This cancellation led to the censure of the university by the American Association of University

Professors[1] and to the demoralization of many of the faculty members we interviewed during a visit to the campus.

At the long-established and more prestigious institutions visited in this survey, the advent of scientific management cannot yet be said to have worked any fundamental alteration in the relationship between faculty and administration. Other innovations have generally tended to offset the effects of managerial changes like the introduction of computers and the establishment of offices of institutional research. If the president's office has grown in administrative authority, so too has the autonomous strength of individual departments through the negotiation of research contracts, which give these subdivisions a measure of fiscal independence, and through the increased competition for high-quality faculty members brought on by the enrollment surge as well as the research revolution. There has, in short, been a simultaneous operation of centripetal as well as centrifugal forces in the most distinguished educational institutions.

Even in the high-prestige schools, the new techniques of management may have a great deal of utility for a university administrator. It is of vital importance that the state legislature and the tax-paying public be convinced of the soundness of university operations. Hence, as noted in the previous chapter, a large state university is often forced to put on a dramatic show of scientific objectivity in its budgeting process in order to justify its requests for continued support, even though the dramatic props—elaborate formulas, statistical ratios, and so on—may have very little to do with the way in which decisions are actually made within the academic establishment. In such a context the new science of management serves not so much to manage the university as to manage the impression that outsiders have about it.[2]

In short, managerial innovations in higher education have consequences which are considerably more tangled than appearances might indicate. New trappings of management sometimes herald authentic changes in university operation. They sometimes conceal the fact that nothing has really changed at all. The image of quantitative rationality is used to discharge a university's obligations to the state without immediately affecting internal patterns of decision making. But even in the universities where scientific management is introduced primarily for its dramaturgical effects, its continued practice may well influence the internal policy of

[1] "Academic Freedom and Tenure: The University of South Florida," *AAUP Bulletin*, Vol. 50, No. 1 (March, 1964), pp. 44-57.

[2] On the concept of dramaturgy and the management of impression, see Erving Goffman, *The Presentation of Self in Everyday Life* (Edinburgh: University of Edinburgh Social Sciences Research Centre, 1956), and Victor Thompson, *Modern Organization: A General Theory* (New York: Alfred A. Knopf, 1961), pp. 138–51.

public institutions of higher education, as administrators come to believe that their judgments are indeed informed by the light of science.

FROM SECRECY TO PUBLICITY

The collection and dissemination of detailed information about the internal affairs of public institutions of higher learning means that state officials and the community at large are much more aware today than was ever true in the past of the way in which colleges and universities are being operated. Traditionally many academic administrators were as secretive about the details of university affairs as a branch of the armed forces might well be about its most cherished military secrets.

The grounds for this secrecy rested essentially on the notion that certain kinds of university practices could not be satisfactorily explained to the outside world, and that the disclosure of information about such matters would bring a swift cutback in legislative appropriations or other reprisals against public colleges and universities. Subterfuge thus became a characteristic style of university administration. Witness, for example, the following report by T. R. McConnell:

> One of the first things this writer was told when he went to a principal state university nearly twenty-five years ago was never to reveal the hidden costs of research to the Legislature. The largest of these costs is the time used for research by faculty members whose salaries are charged entirely to instruction. With contracts and grants from many sources, a large part of the cost of research in the modern university is budgeted under, or charged to "organized research." But a substantial expenditure is still represented by unallocated faculty research time. . . . The fear that in a period of financial stringency legislatures will curtail appropriations for research if expenditures for this purpose are fully revealed is not irrational, of course.[3]

Needless to say, this method of operation aroused considerable suspicion among state legislators and budget officers, and in the past it has been a source of acrimonious dispute between universities and state agencies. In a study in which the authors participated several years ago, we found widespread resentment by state officials against what they regarded as the inordinate secrecy of university administrators.

> In California, for example, the story is told of one meeting with a legislative committee at which the business officer of the university supplied information about the fiscal affairs of the school by referring to a little black book that he kept on his knees out of sight of the legislators present. Irritated by this procedure, one legislator finally demanded that the committee be allowed access to this hidden document. This request was rejected by the business officer on the grounds that it was the only copy he had. . . .

[3] T. R. McConnell, *A General Pattern for American Public Higher Education* (New York: McGraw-Hill, 1962), pp. 108–9.

> Of course there can be no question but that the schools do have grounds for their reluctance to disclose information. In many cases their experience has been that information supplied in good faith has come home to roost in the form of control. There is an abiding fear among many college officials that if they submit budgets in detail it will lead legislatures to pass itemized appropriation acts. Others argue that disclosure brings control over areas of educational policy that have previously been immune from interference.[4]

Along with this tendency to isolate their internal affairs from scrutiny by the outside world, institutions of higher education have also placed a great many restrictions on the free flow of information within the campus itself. In their stimulating analysis of academic culture, Caplow and McGee stress the importance of "information screens" which prevent, inhibit, or distort communications between one segment of a university and another.[5] Departments are understandably reluctant to reveal to administrators or to other departments information on teaching loads, student drop-outs, or any topic which may be subject to unflattering interpretations from their own point of view. Administrators, on the other hand, have long been accustomed to withhold data on an equally wide range of topics. Salary differentials are a particularly sensitive item, with respect both to variations between faculty and administrative staff and among individual academic departments. As noted earlier, this reluctance to permit the free exchange of information has handicapped the operation of institutional research agencies on a number of campuses.[6]

In recent years, however, there has been a persistent trend toward a much more "open" style of university administration. This has been true with respect to both the disclosure of information to the outside world and the modification or elimination of some of the traditional "information screens" that have existed within the academic community. As far as external patterns of communication are concerned, the chief force for change has been the growing pressure from outside organizations for more precise data on the way in which institutions of higher education use their resources. In the case of public institutions this pressure comes from legislatures and other official bodies upon which state colleges and universities depend for financial assistance. But private institutions are subject to similar demands from agencies of the federal government or private philanthropic foundations from which grants or other forms of financial support are being requested. It is fair to say that as a result of his obligation to justify their financial needs many institutions of higher education have discovered details about their own operations that even

[4] Moos and Rourke, *The Campus and the State*, p. 88.

[5] Theodore Caplow and Reece J. McGee, *The Academic Marketplace* (New York: Basic Books, 1958), pp. 59–62.

[6] See pp. 55–57.

their most knowledgeable administrative officers may not have known a few years ago.

The new age of publicity in the development of the university's relations with the outside world is the product not only of this increased demand for accountability but also of the fact that much more efficient machinery and techniques for gathering information have now been developed. The advent of institutional research, electronic data-processing equipment, and the techniques of analyzing budgets and space utilization described in previous chapters have opened up broad new possibilities for organizational self-study on the part of colleges and universities. As a consequence institutions of higher education today not only need to know more but they can know more about what they are doing with their resources than has ever before been the case.

The shift from secrecy to publicity in the style of academic administration carries with it many potential embarrassments for colleges and universities. One midwestern school recently found that a space utilization study it had released to the public soon became a weapon in the hands of opponents of the university's plans for building expansion, since it inevitably revealed less than full use of existing capacity. Another institution in the East avoided a similar fate only by withholding the publication of a space survey which showed a very low rate of utilization of the university's physical plant until it could improve its performance in this regard. Thereupon it conducted and released the findings of a new and much more favorable report.

To a very considerable extent, state colleges and universities push each other in the direction of being much more public than was true in the past since cost and other quantitative studies conducted at one institution very quickly become models for the kind of reports which state officials expect to receive from other schools. While this is particularly true where a number of institutions compete for support in the same state, public institutions of higher education today are becoming increasingly subject to having their performance compared with that of schools in other states, through studies conducted by national, and particularly regional, associations to which they belong. Regional organizations like the Western Interstate Commission on Higher Education (WICHE), the Southern Regional Education Board (SREB), and the New England Board for Higher Education (NEBHE) have played a vital role in stimulating self-analysis and disclosure by institutions in states located within their jurisdiction.

Of great importance also in this respect has been the influence of national associations in which state officials participate. A great deal of information on public higher education today is borne from state to state or currents which have their source at annual conferences of such groups as the National Association of State Budget Officers, where fiscal administrators meet to compare problems and to trade information on possible solutions to difficulties arising in connection with a wide range of state programs, including not least of all in recent years higher education. The internal affairs of public institutions of higher education thus receive greater publicity today not only in the sense of being exposed to closer surveillance within their own state, but also because they are open to scrutiny before a regional or even a national audience.

One index of this trend toward a more open style of university administration is the changing policy of university alumni publications with respect to occurrences on campus that seem to put the university in a bad light—student riots or some *cause célèbre* involving what the community regards as heresy on the part of a professor. In former days it was standard practice to do everything possible to hush up events of this sort—to bury them as far out of sight as the university could manage. Increasingly now universities are taking the lead in presenting a complete and factual account in their own publications of controversial episodes on campus. One of the fullest and most candid reports of the student riots on the University of California's Berkeley campus in 1964 was presented in that university's alumni magazine. In 1965 the Yale alumni magazine published a detailed story on the clash between the university and the student body over the failure of a highly popular philosophy professor to obtain academic tenure.

In no small measure the development of this policy of candor reflects the movement of a new kind of personnel into alumni publications work. In the old days this task was largely performed by old grads with a filiopietistic attitude toward their own institutions, who would have regarded it as sacrilegious to publicize any hint of discord within their alma mater. Now professionals have moved into this area of employment—individuals trained in writing, journalism, or one of the other communications skills. These specialists recognize that bad news cannot be suppressed in a day in which the media of mass circulation are quick to publicize newsworthy events on college campuses. The only rational course of action open to a university faced with a campus crisis of one sort or another is to get its own version of a controversial episode into print as quickly as possible, if for no other reason than to counter exaggerations and distortions that may crop up in other reports and stir apprehensions among parents, alumni, donors, and other constituency groups.

The obstacles to the exchange of information within a university community are even more difficult to remove than those which have traditionally impeded the free flow of communications between the university and the outside community. These barriers are rooted in the self-interest of a variety of competing and strongly entrenched departments and administrative units, each one of which shares a common interest in preserving its own autonomy. These organizations commonly equate autonomy with the retention of a monopoly of information about their own internal affairs. However, each of the trends discussed in previous chapters—the growth of institutional research, the establishment of centralized information systems with electronic data-processing equipment, and the emergence of more refined techniques for measuring and comparing costs and space utilization—are forces working toward an eventual breakdown of traditional information screens within the academic community. A university that has become considerably more "open" in its dealings with the outside world can hardly expect to keep a tight lid on the flow of information internally.

The lowering of information barriers within the university community can have a highly centralizing effect, insofar as it enables top administrative personnel to gain information about schools and departments which enhances their ability to control these subordinate units. This is true, however, only as long as the central administrators are able at the same time to retain restrictions on the flow of data back to the departments. If departments are given unrestricted access to information in a dean's files on comparative salaries within a university, or differentials in teaching loads among academic units, then the less-favored departments may be able to use this information to strengthen their own position in bargaining with the administration. In the light of these considerations it is not surprising that, in the institutions at which our interviews were conducted, individual departments were commonly denied access to any information in a dean's or academic vice-president's office which might incite such interdepartmental jealousy.

It should be noted that this shift from secrecy to publicity in university administration does not necessarily mean the adoption of a policy of greater candor on the part of an institution of higher education. Sometimes it merely reflects adherence to the ancient maxim that there is more than one way to skin a cat. It was reported at one university that a new director of institutional research moved swiftly to abandon the school's traditional policy of concealing information from the legislature and began instead to saturate the state assembly with elaborate analyses of university operations. It was not very long before the chairman of the principal committee dealing with higher education in the legislature was calling the IR director on the phone to beg him not to send in any more reports. In this instance the means had changed but the school's goal of keeping the legislature in the dark remained the same.

THE RISE OF CABINET GOVERNMENT

The shift toward a more "open" style of administration has been accompanied by a modification in the administrative structure at the larger institutions of higher education. More and more the task of managing internal university affairs has been delegated to an assortment of vice-presidents in charge of such matters as business, student, or academic affairs. As a result a new layer of top-level officials has become firmly fixed at the summit of the administrative hierarchy.[7] Where once he reigned in solitary splendor, the university president has now come to share responsibility for governing his institution with a variety of other executive colleagues.

Of central importance here is the fact that these vice-presidents commonly sit together with the president in an executive cabinet, which meets on a regular basis to handle most of the major decisions that come before the university, including budgetary allocations, plans for campus expansion, and other matters of a critical nature. Sometimes this cabinet is very formal in character—an administrative council, budget committee, or some other decision-making body explicitly provided for in the constitution or bylaws of the university. Very often, however, it is a highly informal arrangement—a "kitchen cabinet" of advisors with whom the president habitually meets to discuss the university's most pressing problems.

Paralleling the situation which exists in governmental practice in this country, an official cabinet body and an unofficial kitchen cabinet may co-exist on the same campus, even though their relationship may sometimes be an uneasy one. One institution we visited was governed by a dual cabinet system, known on the campus itself as "the big troika" and "the little troika." The big troika was made up of older executives whose power derived from their official position, the president in association with the treasurer and the provost. The little troika, on the other hand, consisted of three younger administrators who met with the president informally to discuss what they regarded as critical issues facing the university.

In a situation of this kind the kitchen cabinet may become in effect a "war cabinet," which meets to deal with the major strategic issues facing the president, while the formal cabinet handles the more routine issues of policy that arise in the day-to-day life of the university. The existence of

[7] The question of how large an institution has to be before it needs such a layer of vice-presidents is a moot one. At one institution we visited, the charge was made that the president had appointed more vice-presidents than the school actually needed in order to keep in step with the larger institutions.

this war cabinet device has been particularly important for public universities faced with the problem of rapid growth—especially where it has required the development of new campuses. The political pressures the university confronts may be intense; crises in relations with the legislature, a state co-ordinating board for higher education, or its own trustees may flare up at any moment. The war cabinet is thus an administrative response to a situation of environment in flux in which emergencies become almost routine.

This new pattern of cabinet government stands in sharp contrast to the administrative tradition of higher education, which is so distinctively "presidential" in its general orientation. Histories of colleges and universities in this country commonly trace the development of their subject in terms of the men who have successively occupied the office of president. Very often there is a nostalgia for the days of the great educational leaders of the past—the nineteenth-century hero-presidents who founded an institution or lifted it to its first renown. To a very considerable extent these early presidents have become models by which their contemporary successors have been measured and found wanting. Criticism of the modern day university president has focused very much on the fact that he is, more often than not, an administrative caretaker rather than an academic trail blazer in higher education.[8]

The passing of the heroic style of leadership is by no means unique to higher education. It is in fact quite similar to changes which have occurred in other forms of organization. Students of the military, for example, have noted the shift in that sphere of activity from the warrior to a managerial style of leadership.[9] Increasingly, military command gravitates to the officer who has demonstrated his mastery of organizational rather than battlefield skills. In the same way, the university president is now required not so much to be an innovator in matters of education as to be an effective manager of a vast and complex educational enterprise.

In this context the emergence of the cabinet system of government in university administration simply reflects the necessities imposed by size and complexity. The president becomes a prime minister because he no longer can administer the university alone. The management of business firms went through a somewhat similar process earlier in this country, as in the course of time business firms moved out from the control of individual free-wheeling entrepreneurs into the jurisdiction of executive

[8] See Harold W. Dodds, *The Academic President—Educator or Caretaker?* (New York: McGraw-Hill, 1962).

[9] In this connection see Morris Janowitz, *The Professional Soldier* (New York: The Free Press of Glencoe, 1960).

committees.[10] In spite of the long-standing tendency in organization theory to disparage such plural executive arrangements, universities like other organizations have found it necessary once they reach an advanced stage to establish systems of governance in which the chief executive shares authority over decision making with other officials. The range of subjects over which decision must now range is so vast as to demand the advantages of division of labor in the performance of the executive function as well as in the other tasks of large organizations.

The emergence of the cabinet system by no means implies the abdication of the president from a position of central responsibility in the government of the university, for the role of prime minister is itself a powerful one, as the experience of parliamentary government clearly testifies. Even if a university president were no more than a prime minister, his responsibility with respect to the trustees and his authority in the eyes of the faculty are sources of influence no other university executive can match. In point of fact, a university president is far more than a prime minister. The only certain power which the cabinet as a whole has over him is that of giving advice, which he may or may not choose to accept. The university cabinet is patterned much more closely after the model of American rather than British government, and American presidents have been notoriously unwilling to have their decisions determined by cabinet vote. Typical perhaps was the situation at one university where it was said that if a cabinet vote went 6–1 against a president, he might very well be influenced by it, but if the vote were only 4–3 against him, he would be as likely as not to ignore it.

Certainly it is true that no university official is in a better position than a president to stimulate or enhance capacities for academic achievement on campus. True enough, the modern university president does not himself tend to be an innovator in the same sense as the giants of the past —Eliot at Harvard, Gilman at Hopkins, or Angell at Michigan—but the role of these past presidents was often conditioned by the presence of a unique historical situation: the founding of a university. The presidents who take over existing institutions today have no equal opportunity to impress their own will on their environment. But even if modern university presidents are not themselves trail blazers, their influence goes a long way toward determining whether or not trails are blazed on campus. One university in our sample has begun to take a great leap forward during the past decade precisely because its president has been able to

[10] See Alfred D. Chandler, Jr., and Fritz Redlich, "Recent Developments in American Business Administration and Their Conceptualization," *Business History Review*, Vol. 35 (Spring, 1961), pp. 9–15.

play a catalytic role in stimulating renewal and innovation in the individual academic departments.

What a university president has most to fear from the rise of cabinet government is the development of a direct relationship between one of his executive colleagues and the trustees, which in effect removes a sphere of authority from presidential control. The only area in which this problem looms at all large on the administrative horizon today is with respect to finance, for trustee committees on a number of campuses have developed a direct tie with a financial vice-president or some other chief fiscal officer. Quite often this relationship centers on fiscal management problems, such as the handling of the university's endowment portfolio. If the connection of the fiscal vice-president with the trustees were in time to embrace wider areas of policy, or if a parallel relationship were to develop with all the other vice-presidents, then a university president might indeed soon find himself relegated to the position of the constitutional monarch who "reigns but does not govern."

There have also been misgivings on some campuses regarding the extent to which the existence of the cabinet acts to cut the president off from the faculty, department chairmen, deans, or indeed from grass-roots sentiment on the campus generally. From this perspective the cabinet is viewed as a bottleneck in the system of university communications. One way in which a president can overcome any such isolating effect that a cabinet may have is to assign special assistants in his own office to the task of keeping channels of communication open to all segments of the university community. These presidential aides can also serve to keep the power of the vice-presidents in check by acting to provide the president with his own source of advice and information outside of the cabinet system.

In this respect the executive assistants of a university president play much the same role as the chief White House aides to a U.S. president, keeping a chief executive from becoming in effect a captive of his own bureaucracy and helping to preserve his freedom of action and decision. At the University of Oregon the office of the president is a highly developed administrative apparatus; there is considerable feeling on campus that this organizational pattern can be traced to the background of the university president, who spent considerable time in Washington in high positions with the Eisenhower administration. One other advantage which a group of executive aides may have for a university president is that they are his own appointees, while many of the other members of his official family are individuals he inherited when he took office.

The number of offices included within a university cabinet varies considerably from one campus to another, since there are virtually as many administrative patterns for governing institutions of higher education as there are colleges and universities in this country. University vice-presidents, for example, have a wide range of responsibilities, for there is no agreed-upon set of functions which this layer of executives should perform. The proliferation of vice-presidents which has occurred at this level of administration was amusingly illustrated on one campus when the president could not recall the names of all his vice-presidents in the course of an interview with one of the authors.

However varied the duties of vice-presidents may be, there are two quite distinct sets of interests or viewpoints which must find representation or expression in any cabinet system. One is the academic or educational perspective, and the other is the fiscal or housekeeping point of view. These contrasting outlooks are usually represented by an academic vice-president on the one hand, and a financial vice-president on the other. Virtually all major decisions on university policy turn ultimately on some resolution of the inherent conflict between a university's objectives and its capacities. The cabinet is often the major institutional mechanism through which a president can weigh and balance his commitment to academic excellence with his responsibility for fiscal solvency, as these conflicting needs are articulated by their chief administrative protagonists —the academic and fiscal vice-presidents.

DECISION MAKING IN HIGHER EDUCATION

The ultimate goal of the new techniques of management is to enable colleges and universities to make more rational decisions about the use of their own resources and the direction of their development. The extent to which this expectation has been fulfilled in higher education is as yet far from clear, for these techniques are still in their infancy in most colleges and universities. But it is possible at this point to make a preliminary assessment of the way in which the new science of management influences the actual decisions made by institutions of higher learning, recognizing at the same time that judgments in many areas must still be highly tentative.

One conclusion which the data presented in previous chapters have made abundantly clear is that the instruments of rationalized management have had much more effect upon the routine day-to-day organizational decisions in colleges and universities than they have upon the novel, nonrecurring decisions of academic life. This has been true with respect to each of the diverse areas that discussion has touched on—institutional research, the use of computers in administration, and resource allocation. Using the distinction formulated by Herbert Simon, it would be correct to say that the new techniques have exerted their greatest influence in programed rather than nonprogramed areas of decision,[11] or in Selznick's terminology, the routine rather than the critical choices of organizational life.[12]

This finding needs, however, to be qualified at this point by one important consideration. In actuality it is not always possible to separate the routine from the critical in a perfectly categorical way. A changing pattern of routine decisions in an area like student admissions can, in cumulative effect, bring about a major shift in university policy. If, for example, a set of new routines introduced by the admissions office succeeds in identifying and bringing to the university a much improved quality of student body, then the whole level of academic performance at the institution may be markedly raised without any high-level decision to this effect having been made at all. Or, if a new pattern of course scheduling wrought by the introduction of computers into space allocation gives priority to teaching rather than to research needs, then again a major change in the character of an institution has occurred without any conscious decision by an administrator. What these possibilities suggest, of course, is that changes in routine may sometimes have unintended consequences of a critical nature. Hence the eventual effects of the new techniques of management upon higher education may not prove to be as purely procedural or routine as some administrators may at first believe.

One of the expected advantages of using quantitative methods in university management is that the use of these techniques, especially where automation is involved, will relieve administrators of the chore of routine decision making and leave them free to devote their energies to the more important "critical" levels of policy. It has been pointed out that administrators who have both routine and critical responsibilities to discharge often allow their time to be monopolized by the task of handling routine decisions, presumably because answers to these routine problems are much easier to come by than are solutions to novel, nonrecurring difficulties.[13] It is not unreasonable then to expect that as the new science of management takes over the burden of routine decision it will shift the attention of top-level university officials to critical areas of concern.

Moreover, the new methods generate a good deal more information on university operations than was previously available, thus alerting administrators to many critical situations where decisions may have to be made.

[11] Simon, *The New Science of Management Decision*, pp. 5–8.

[12] Philip Selznick, *Leadership in Administration* (Evanston, Ill.: Row, Peterson, 1957), pp. 29–64.

[13] See James G. March and Herbert A. Simon, *Organizations* (New York: John Wiley, 1958), pp. 185–87. This is somewhat analogous to Parkinson's law of triviality—"the time spent on any item of the agenda will be inversely proportional to the sum involved." C. Northcote Parkinson, *Parkinson's Law* (Boston: Houghton Mifflin, 1962), p. 24.

Institutional research, for example, when it is operating effectively, can force items onto the agenda of decision by providing university officials with information on a wide range of important problems that they may not have even known about before. While the new science of management may lighten the burden of routine decision, therefore, it may also increase the responsibility of university officials for making critical choices in many areas where matters might previously have been allowed merely to drift.

Eventually this revolution in data gathering may push colleges and universities in the direction of much more self-conscious concern for long-range planning. In the past, the development of institutions of higher education has been very much a response to the pressures and opportunities to which they were subject. Such strategy as they have followed in institutional planning might best be described as one of organizational opportunism. Rather than tailoring decisions on their own development to fit a preconceived notion of the kind of institution they wanted to become, colleges and universities have, more often than not, become whatever their situation forced or allowed them to become. Vulnerable as so many of them have been to the withdrawal of financial support, they have been in effect "precarious organizations"—compelled to accommodate to their environment in order to ensure their survival.[14]

To be sure, this has been a highly useful characteristic of institutions of higher education from the point of view of society at large, since it has prevented colleges and universities from isolating themselves from the needs of their environment and has made them highly responsive—as compared at least with European institutions—to the educational needs of the community. Like the economic enterprises which loom so large on the American scene, colleges and universities have been strongly "market-oriented." At the same time, however, this highly adaptive characteristic of American institutions of higher learning has also reflected their lack of explicit consideration of where their decisions were taking them and whether or not they wanted to go in this direction. The new techniques of management at least enhance the ability of colleges and universities to engage in systematic foresight, if they choose to do so.

One hypothesis entertained at the outset of this study was that the new techniques of management would bring a new type of machine-tooled decision maker into positions of leadership in university administration. These new men of power would be skilled in computer technology, quanti-

[14] In this regard see Burton R. Clark, "Organizational Adaptation and Precarious Values: A Case Study," *American Sociological Review*, Vol. 21 (June, 1956), pp. 327–36. This article puts into a more general theoretical framework a case study by Clark of a precarious organization, *Adult Education in Transition: A Study of Institutional Insecurity* (Berkeley: University of California Press, 1956).

tative research, or some other facet of the new science of management. We found no evidence to support this hypothesis.[15] The possession of technical management skills does not seem to open up any royal road to advancement in higher education. Whatever power the director of a computer center or an IR office may acquire in his own right, such positions do not themselves tend to be stepping stones to higher office.

What is happening instead is that top-level administrators are themselves becoming more quantitatively oriented, much more interested than they once were in creating and drawing on the staff services which institutional research and computer centers can provide. One university official commented that while the new science of management was not bringing any "new men" to the fore, it was developing a somewhat different side of the men with traditional backgrounds who were continuing to move into university administration. A striking indication of this new orientation by top-level administrators is the evidence that colleges and universities are much more willing today than they once were to draw on the services of management consulting firms for advice on administrative problems on campus.

One central question which a study of this kind obviously raises is the extent to which the advent of new management techniques is affecting the comparative influence of faculty and administration on the decision-making processes of the university. On the surface the new management science would seem to offer abundant opportunity for the aggrandizement of administrative power. And, as we pointed out earlier, this is precisely what has occurred at some of the newer universities, where there has been a virtual hypertrophy of the administrative process. Sometimes, this overdevelopment of bureaucracy stems from the fact that many of the new universities until recently were teachers colleges and hence are quite acclimated to the notion of administrative dominance characteristic of elementary and secondary school education in this country. Or it may originate simply in the fact that administrative power in the early stages of development on a new campus is not balanced or limited by the opposition of an entrenched faculty.

In established universities, however, administrative and faculty power is subject to an elaborate system of checks and balances, and this equilib-

[15] See, for example, Appendix B, pp. 150–54, where an analysis of the background of college and university presidents shows no tendency for these executives to be drawn from managerial rather than educational backgrounds. In fact, the data clearly show that the overwhelming majority of presidents have some kind of academic background.

This analysis also turned up some interesting regional variations with respect to chief executives. The presidents of southern institutions are most likely to be natives of their own region and the presidents of western schools are least likely to be. See Table B–24.

rium tends to be somewhat self-sustaining. It is true, as noted in the discussion of computers as well as space allocation, that a shift in decision-making authority from academic departments to central administrators may occur as a result of the introduction of new managerial techniques. At the same time, however, there may still be enough slack in the system of control that the faculty is able to retain many of its traditional prerogatives. Or the loss in power sustained by departments may be offset by a gain for faculty members appointed to committees newly established to oversee the activities of an institutional research bureau, or to engage in long-range planning for the university. While some faculty members, especially department chairmen, may lose power as a result of the new management procedures, others may gain in influence.

Actually a clear dichotomy between the faculty on the one hand and administration on the other simply does not exist at most institutions of higher education today. Campus politics are far more complicated than that. There are often sharp cleavages between administrative offices themselves in their attitudes toward the new managerial innovations as on other matters. The faculty too is often divided on the issue. On one campus we visited, which is transforming itself from a municipal teachers' college into a major state university, the chairman of one department commented that he would oppose any effort to give the faculty a stronger voice in university government. In his judgment there were still far too many holdovers on the faculty from the teacher-training days, who were not at all interested in research or in making the university a first-rate scholarly institution. The administration, on the other hand, was quite energetic in its pursuit of the goal of higher academic standing for the institution. Contrary to what a great many faculty members devoutly believe, there are institutions of higher education in this country where it is the administrators who have taken the lead in pressing for academic excellence.

As far as the effects of the new science of management on faculty-administration relations are concerned, it may well be the case that substantial segments of university operation can be subjected to rationalization without disturbing the areas of academic decision subject to faculty control that lie at the heart of a university's existence. As Harold Leavitt points out, organizations today are increasingly subject to internal differentiation in their management practices, and there is no reason why a single style of administration has to prevail in all areas of institutional operation. Witness the fact that research and development units in industrial concerns can be freed from many of the routines and controls that govern other areas of the firm's activity. As Leavitt puts it, "While the creative researcher is being left free to create, the materials purchasing clerk must conform more tightly than ever to the new computer controlled program that he has been handed."[16]

Certainly there is no intrinsic reason why this same kind of internal differentiation cannot prevail in universities as well, with the important aspects of teaching and research left entirely free from administrative rationalization while the computers take over such matters as student registration, payrolls, and space allocation. But it is important to note that the process of rationalization does create within universities a greatly enhanced potential for administrative dominance in colleges and universities. There is perhaps a parallel here with the situation in Republican France prior to World War II, where a system of democratic politics and administrative absolutism remained in uneasy co-existence—with the threat never entirely absent that the bureaucracy would move in and assume sole sovereignty over the machinery of government. Clearly, if the faculty is to retain anything like the traditional scope of its power in a rationalized university, it will need to develop more effective techniques for participating in university government than the town-meeting devices that have been standard procedure in the past.

THE MULTI-CAMPUS UNIVERSITY

The advent of the new science of management holds out special promise and simultaneously poses difficult issues in a setting where a number of campuses are linked together in a single statewide system of higher education. A multi-campus university is distinct in several ways from a single-campus institution, and the same factors which have made the multi-campus university especially fertile ground for experimentation with new techniques of management also create resistance to managerial innovation.

First and foremost, the multi-campus university is geographically dispersed, which makes it both more necessary and more difficult for a central administration to guide, monitor, or even to communicate with local campuses. Secondly, each local campus usually has its own fully developed administrative apparatus paralleling the administrative offices at the statewide level and creating problems of redundancy and co-ordination. Finally, the traditional conflict in academic administration over centralization and decentralization is much more acute in a multi-campus environment. In a single-campus university, conflict over the degree of administrative centralization that is necessary is usually confined within the campus community. Where more than one campus is involved, and where each of these campuses is in formidable competition with the other

[16] See Harold J. Leavitt, "Unhuman Organizations," *Harvard Business Review*, Vol. 40 (July–August, 1962), pp. 90–98.

and serves a distinct regional clientele, the division of authority between the central office and the local campus can easily become a matter of public and political conflict within the state.

Nowhere are the issues of multi-campus management more dramatically illustrated than in the University of California, whose nine campuses are scattered throughout the state, and where the academic and administrative objectives of the local campuses are often at variance with the central university administration. While the demonstrations which broke out on the Berkeley campus in 1964 were rooted in student grievances in the sphere of politics rather than administration, the efforts to explain and prevent a recurrence of these outbreaks came ultimately to focus on the need for reform in the managerial procedures and relationships which had previously prevailed in the multi-campus system.

In its aggravated form, the multi-campus problem in California is a comparatively recent phenomenon. For fifty years after the founding of the University of California in 1868, the Berkeley campus was virtually synonymous with the university as a whole.[17] What is now the University of California at Los Angeles became a part of the university system in 1919, offering the first significant challenge to the primacy of Berkeley within the university system. And as UCLA began its drive for growth and quality, it was joined after 1944 by a rapid progression of new campuses at Santa Barbara, Davis, and Riverside. At the present time still other campuses are going into operation as fast as buildings can be put up at Santa Cruz, Irvine, and San Diego.

In the University of California system, geographical dispersal creates major problems of central direction. The physical distance between campuses in California forces administrators to spend an inordinate amount of time traveling around the state in order to maintain personal contact within the system. A variety of devices has been employed to keep the campuses in closer touch with each other and with the central office. Open-line telephones between many of the offices permit administrators to talk with each other as if they were on the same campus. Eventually, integrated computer systems may tie together computer units on local campuses with a central computer facility so that information processed locally can be monitored or analyzed almost simultaneously by the central offices. But at the present time, administrators in the University

[17] The San Francisco Medical School was established in 1873, while agricultural stations were established at Davis and Riverside early in the century. For a review of the chronology see Liaison Committee of the California State Board of Education and the Regents of the University of California, *A Study of the Need for Additional Centers for Public Higher Education in California* (Sacramento: California State Department of Education, 1957), pp. 21 ff.

of California system are generally agreed that the central office cannot exercise uniform surveillance over the different campuses. Some officials on the Berkeley campus, for example, feel that the central office keeps a closer watch on Berkeley's operations than it does on the operations of other campuses simply because the central office is located next to the Berkeley campus.

In California as in other multi-campus systems the central administrative structure is duplicated by administrations on each campus. For example, the president and vice-presidents at the statewide office are paralleled by chancellors and vice-chancellors on the individual campuses. A central budget office is matched by local budget offices. Now, partly in response to the existence of a central office of institutional research, local campuses in the University of California system are beginning to develop their own institutional research offices. This multiple layering of administrative officials may be an unavoidable consequence of growth in size (although the point is hotly debated), but it is also a common source of conflict. The number of layers in the hierarchy makes vertical communication extremely difficult. Messages tend to become blurred on their way up or down the administrative hierarchy, and even when communication is reasonably clear, local administrators may still evade the intentions of the central office.

In a multi-campus setting, an inordinate amount of time must also be spent in working out agreements between counterpart officials. To some observers, the multi-campus university inevitably becomes a parody of bureaucracy in which the appearance of an administrative office at one level begets a new office at another level, and these new offices then devote their primary energies to talking to each other.

Recently the issue of centralization versus decentralization came to a head in California with the publication of a report on the Berkeley riots in 1964. This report, commissioned by the trustees and prepared by a special investigating committee under the direction of Jerome C. Byrne, was a stinging attack upon the administrative policies of the regents, the president, and the local administrators of the Berkeley campus.[18] The Byrne report said bluntly that the regents had tried to control too much, that the central administration was in a state of chaos, and that there was a serious lack of quality leadership at all levels of university affairs.

The essential recommendation of the Byrne commission was for a radical delegation of authority in university affairs to the local campuses. Ironically, this recommendation seemed to have little bearing on the

[18] Jerome C. Byrne *et al.*, *Report on the University of California and Recommendations to the Special Committee of the Regents of the University of California* (Berkeley, mimeo., May 7 ,1965).

diagnosis made in the first part of the report, for the report had criticized the quality of administration at the local levels as strongly as it had criticized the central administrators. The inarticulate premise of the report was that a loose confederation of autonomous institutions would be in a better position to preserve the essential requisites of free inquiry and speech than an institution governed more centrally—an intriguing echo of anti-federalist arguments during the debates over the ratification of the American Constitution. Put another way, the report appeared to assume that poor administration on one campus might not be as fatal to a free university as poor administration from a central point. Conversely, the report seemed to imply that no amount of effective administration from a central point would offset the potential dangers arising from overcentralization.

Local campuses, especially Berkeley and UCLA, seized upon the Byrne report as a mandate for emancipation from the controls of the statewide office. Under pressure from these campuses, but partly as an outgrowth of his own philosophy, President Kerr responded with a set of recommendations which represented a middle ground between the existing centralized practices and the proposals for almost total decentralization advocated in the Byrne report.[19]

President Kerr called upon the regents to delegate further authority to each campus in matters of academic planning, teaching, student life, physical development, and administrative organization. He proposed a system whereby the statewide administration would review campus operations for effectiveness, but would refrain as much as possible from day-to-day control over those operations. He further suggested that the local campuses decentralize their own internal operations, giving deans and department chairmen greater authority than they presently enjoyed.

The Kerr recommendations, like all others, could scarcely be regarded as a panacea for the administrative ills of such a mammoth university system. President Kerr recognized this in the opening statement of his proposals when he said, "The organization of the University of California has been and should continue to be subject to constant study and open to evolutionary change whenever change will improve its functioning."[20]

Our purpose here is not to suggest a conclusion to the unfinished story of the University of California. Like so many other great universities in the United States, it will continue to experiment, to adjust, and to experience conflict within the academic community. It will try out new styles of management yet ungenerated, as it has tried out the systems we have

[19] University of California, *University Bulletin*, Vol. 13, No. 38, (June 1, 1965), pp. 239–40.

[20] *Ibid.*, p. 239.

been describing in this study. Managerial techniques, new arrangements of administrative officers, new divisions of authority between the central office and the local campuses are almost inevitably going to be a major part of the future history of the university. Certainly one of the great unresolved questions at this university—and in this study—is whether the new techniques of management inexorably force a centralization of power in spite of the intent or desire on the part of officials themselves to decentralize authority within the academic community.

Chapter Six

THE MEANING OF MANAGERIAL INNOVATION

Up to this point we have confined ourselves to identifying the new managerial patterns that have emerged in institutions of higher education. Computers, institutional research, and the other instruments and avenues of managerial science have been examined from the point of view of their origins, the kind of utility they have in the operation of colleges and universities, and the effects these new tools of management have on decision making and the distribution of influence among various groups in the academic community. The orientation of this discussion has been descriptive and analytical.

Although we realize it is early to pass any final judgments, this last chapter presents a more normative and subjective assessment of managerial innovation. We would like in a brief way to appraise the meaning or implications of what we have observed under three headings: (1) the aspects of the new managerial science that we believe point in the right direction and are most worthy of imitation by institutions of higher education generally; (2) certain pitfalls into which administrators may easily be led by hasty or uncritical use of the new techniques of management; and (3) problems in the government of colleges and universities that the new science of management has brought to the fore and that have not yet been squarely faced in higher education.

PATHS TO THE FUTURE

Easily the most noteworthy feature of the managerial revolution in higher education is that it has not led to the universal triumph of any Gresham's law of administration. The soft currency of quantitative standards has not in fact driven out qualitative criteria altogether in the management of colleges and universities. In the recruitment of top-level administrators, for example, it is still generally the case that the qualities which institutions of the first rank look for in positions of leadership are such intangible skills as the ability to look ahead, to anticipate change, to handle with diplomacy relations with the outside world or disputes and disagreements within the university community itself. This kind of leadership skill, involving personal qualities and the capacity for judgment, is still infinitely more important than sheer technical ability as a prerequisite for administrative leadership in higher education.

As we have noted, the tendency toward overly zealous or premature commitment to the newer techniques of management seems largely to be localized at the newer universities with rapidly swelling enrollments. These universities are either newly established or recently converted from the status of teachers' college or agricultural school. However, in many instances this tendency toward the overdevelopment of administration at the emerging universities may be no more than a transitional phenomenon. If these campuses develop toward first-class university status they will inevitably begin to acquire the characteristics of quality institutions. Academic background will become increasingly important in the selection of top-rank administrators, and zeal for the new science of management will have to be tempered by concern for maintaining a lively intellectual atmosphere in which neither students nor faculty are in a constant state of incipient revolt against the confining restrictions of a bureaucratic campus.

We have also tried to stress the view that the new approach to management should be made relevant to academic goals as well as housekeeping needs wherever possible. While there is always the danger that an institution will make an excessive commitment to quantitative management in areas of academic decision where this approach does not really fit, it is equally important to keep management from measuring only those things which it is convenient to measure, and then giving the resulting calibrations unwarranted weight in the decision-making process. Cost studies, for example, can easily have much more influence than they deserve—to the disadvantage of high-cost programs—if they are not balanced by an equivalent effort to appraise the possibility that much more is being achieved in areas of high-cost than in low-cost operations.

Hence we have argued in our discussion of institutional research for the development of IR offices that are primarily directed toward the achievement of academic goals rather than housekeeping efficiency. A number of such offices are oriented in this academic direction already and it is our conviction that this precedent should be followed by other schools. If we can assume that financial analysis, space planning, and other kinds of self-study into housekeeping operations are being carried on in a business or plant manager's office, then an IR agency can fairly be given primary responsibility for appraising how well an institution is achieving its educational mission.

Finally, in concluding this overview of administrative practices that are worthy of general adoption, we would cite the growing tendency toward candor in the communications systems of universities—especially with respect to the outside community. True enough, as institutions of higher education have long feared, the new processes of communication open up the possibility that outside groups will become more knowledgeable about, and hence conceivably more critical of, the internal operations of a university. But it is also true that the new techniques can be instruments of persuasion in the hands of the university, enabling institutions of higher education to dispel misgivings and doubts in the general public about the effectiveness of their operations. It seems a fair assumption that these two effects will cancel each other out, leaving the university no less autonomous than it was before the day of computers, institutional research, or the program budget.

In any case, a policy of candor offers the prospect of increasing the rationality of university decision. In the process of concealing information from others, universities have often in the past concealed it from themselves, making it much more difficult to make intelligent decisions about their own development. As far as candor is concerned, virtue is not its own, and only, reward. It may also enhance administrative efficiency. But in the interest of candor ourselves, we should also note that the practice of dissembling has by no means vanished from university communications. In one state we visited, it was reported that a leading institution had successfully persuaded the legislature to raise its appropriation by showing that its total student population, based on a head-count, had climbed to 21,000. Shortly thereafter the state college association to which the institution belonged attempted to use this 21,000 figure as a basis for its annual dues assessment. Looking over its shoulder in this direction, the institution in question quickly replied that its real enrollment was of course only 13,000—in terms of full-time-equivalent students.

PITFALLS TO BE AVOIDED

One question which crops up more than any other among those concerned about the impact of the new managerial techniques upon institutions of higher education is the extent to which the introduction of the computer on campus has contributed to impersonality in the handling of students. The notion that such depersonalization is occurring is often reflected in campus newspapers and other avenues for the expression of student opinion as we move into a day in which the computer takes over the processing of student applications, registration procedures, class scheduling, the posting of grades, decisions on dismissal, and other aspects of student life. As a matter of fact, it appears inevitable that in the university of the future virtually every routine administrative contact with the student will be channeled through electronic data-processing equipment.

To be sure, the computer is more the symbol than it is the source of impersonality on campuses today. The source of this impersonality is the growing size of student populations and the sense that the individual student thereby acquires of being a part of a faceless mass of humanity on campus. The computer itself is simply a technological device designed to help administrators cope with this problem of size. But when this much has been said, it still remains true that universities in this country certainly do not do all that they could do to prevent the use of computers from reinforcing the sense of impersonality which the environment of a large campus can easily convey.

Of course many institutions claim to use automatic data-processing equipment to handle routine chores connected with the administration of student affairs so as to free the time and energy of staff members to deal with students on a personal basis. However, an imaginative program for using computers, or the time made available by their use, to relieve the student's sense of impersonality has yet to be put into effect on any of the campuses we visited. As the discussion in Chapter 2 reveals, universities have been unable to avoid the pitfall of having computers aggravate rather than alleviate the negative effects of large size on campus morale.

In our discussion of resource allocation we also suggested that many of the standards that have been developed to govern the allotment of funds or the utilization of buildings are formulas based on convenience, or political necessity, or the tradition of an institution. Unless care is taken, however, these standards may tend over time to be regarded as having some scientific exactitude, especially where they can be expressed in precise quantitative terms. Such formulas may thus have the effect of reducing rather than enhancing rationality in decision making on the part of the university, insofar as institutions give undue weight to quantitative standards that are useful but not necessarily valid. In many of the areas of management in which efforts to measure are being carried on, it still needs to be very much an open question as to what an appropriate empirical standard is. It is certainly not a contribution to rational administration to fix upon such a standard before there is any assurance that the yardstick rests upon a solid foundation. Relevant here is a comment on the fallibility of quantitative data by Sir Josiah Stamp:

> The individual source of the statistics may easily be the weakest link. Harold Cox tells a story of his life as a young man in India. He quoted some statistics to a Judge, an Englishman, and a very good fellow. His friend said, "Cox, when you are a bit older, you will not quote Indian statistics with that assurance. The Government are very keen on amassing

statistics—they collect them, add them, raise them to the nth power, take the cube root and prepare wonderful diagrams. But what you must never forget is that every one of those figures comes in the first instance from the *chowty dar* (village watchman), who just puts down what he damn pleases."[1]

Nowhere in higher education is this story more applicable than it is to the development of standards based on faculty workload studies.

We have also tried to stress the importance of avoiding a dogmatic approach toward the use of the new techniques of management. Institutions of higher education do not have to make an all-or-nothing choice between the explicit, rationalized procedures of the new science of management and the disorderly, unorganized environment traditionally characteristic of academic activity itself. The notion of the "two cultures," which has a variety of applications in higher education, can also mean the co-existence on campus of a sphere of operations centered on housekeeping matters which is tightly rationalized, along with comparatively loose and unstructured arrangements which are retained for teaching and research. This is, as noted earlier, a dichotomy which prevails in many areas of public and private administration today, for it is coming to be much more generally recognized that where research and creativity are important in organizations, true efficiency may require a certain looseness and disorderliness in administrative operations. If the possibility of such organizational dichotomy is recognized in higher education as well, a great deal of the anxiety generated by the new techniques of management will be dissipated.

THE MANAGERIAL REVOLUTION AND UNIVERSITY GOVERNMENT

The managerial revolution also raises important questions with respect to university government that have not yet been adequately recognized by institutions of higher education. Before concluding this study we would like to draw attention to these issues because we believe that in decades to come they will become increasingly important on campuses across the country. These are not problems to which our inquiries were designed to provide solutions, but they are issues that were constantly drawn to our attention as we pursued our investigation of recent managerial innovations in higher education.[2]

[1] Sir Josiah Stamp, *Some Economic Factors in Modern Life* (London: P. S. King, 1929), pp. 258–59. We are indebted to Dr. Elmer West for bringing this quotation to our attention.

[2] These problems are also becoming increasingly important at universities in other societies. See Appendix C for a discussion of managerial developments at universities in European and Commonwealth countries. While there has been no administrative "upheaval" at these schools, the changes that have taken place certainly parallel those that have occurred in the United States.

The central problem of university government which the managerial revolution has highlighted and to no small extent contributed is the question of the participation of the academic staff in the decision-making processes of the university. In the past, faculty participation in university governance has been very largely carried on through what might be called devices of direct democracy. In various ways the faculty as a whole has directly involved itself in the areas of university decision for which the academic staff was conceded to have actual if not legal responsibility. Either through a general assembly or some other avenue of mass participation the faculty has collectively deliberated on matters of policy where its views needed to be consulted.

Now, however, this form of participation has proved to be impractical. As campuses expand and faculty members and disciplines multiply, the large faculty gathering becomes as cumbersome a vehicle of governance as the town meeting in New England has become. It is increasingly necessary to resort to representative devices to assure an effective voice for the faculty in university decision making, a development which parallels changes also taking place in rapidly growing New England towns. This need for representative rather than direct democracy inevitably points the way toward the establishment of executive committees to represent faculty opinion in the framing of educational policy, or acceptance by faculty members of a larger role for academic administrators who will represent their interests in the day-to-day management of university affairs.

The necessity for shifting from direct democracy to representative government is not always recognized by university faculties, however. The most paradoxical development in higher education in recent years has been the fact that the status of the individual faculty member has been growing on university campuses even while his participation in university government has been declining. In the old days the faculty asserted itself by claiming the right to participate in university government. Now, however, there are bigger fish for the academic man to fry on many campuses—research contracts, consultantships, and the other spoils of the affluent academic society. If anything, the individual faculty member now tends to assert his power by declining to participate in university government. Unless effective channels for representing the views of the faculty in university government are maintained, however, control over internal academic policy will be left entirely in the hands of business administrators. This trend will follow not from administrative design or aggrandizement, but as a result of faculty default. From the point of view of the efficiency of the university, this will be a highly undesirable development, not because it violates any inalienable right of the faculty to control academic affairs, but simply because on academic matters faculty advice is essential to the development of relevant university policy.

What we are suggesting here is that the faculty must modernize its own organization to cope with the changes that have occurred in the business aspects of university administration. Throughout modern society there has been a trend toward the growth of executive power resulting from the increasing need for speed of decision and continuity of attention to the critical problems on the agenda of all organizations. College and university faculties must come to terms with this trend by creating and delegating authority to committees and individuals empowered to represent the faculty point of view in the on-going business of a university. If a faculty is to be influential in the affairs of a university it must be able to decide as well as to deliberate. And faculties today are not as well organized for decision and action as they are for deliberation.

A revolution on the management side of higher education thus calls for a revolution in the academic sphere. Often in the past faculties have put themselves in the indefensible position of being willing neither to assume the burden of guiding a university's academic development nor to concede to others the right to do so. The faculty role in university government is often less than it should be in many areas of policy. This power can be effectively asserted on a day-to-day basis only by a continuously functioning instrumentality, either a faculty committee or a cadre of academic administrators. Indeed, the most effective response by the faculty to the bureaucratization of the university today may well be the development of its own academic civil service, which will reflect faculty rather than administrative points of view in the management of the university.

Appendix A

A NOTE ON RESEARCH STRATEGY

At the outset of this study we stated that we were trying to do two things: (1) to chart the extent to which new managerial practices have been introduced in higher education, and (2) to assess the effects of these innovations on the operation of academic institutions. In planning the course of our investigation we decided that these two objectives would require quite different approaches in our research.

To obtain detailed information on new management practices, such as the roster of offices of institutional research already established or the number of institutions using program budgets, we relied primarily on a mailed four-part questionnaire. Questionnaires were sent to all the four-year, state-supported colleges and universities (361 were listed in the *Education Directory, 1963–64, Part 3*) and to a sample of 36 nonstate public institutions and 36 private institutions. This same schedule of questions was also sent to ten statewide co-ordinating boards.

Returns were received from 290 state colleges and universities—almost exactly an 80 per cent response—and from about the same proportion of the other institutions and boards included in the survey. In 10 per cent of the returns, one or more parts of the questionnaire were blank or unusable, which accounts for differences in the base figures among various tables presented in the previous chapters.

We had some fear that the institutions failing to answer the questionnaire would be of a particular size or region, thereby giving us a distorted picture of national practices. Happily, however, the institutions that did not answer reflected about the same distribution in size and region as those that did respond, giving us considerable confidence in the summary data. Appendix B presents a statistical analysis of the questionnaire returns.

Valuable as these questionnaires proved to be, they could not reveal the actual effects of new management practices in higher education. A return might show, for example, that a university used computers for certain administrative activities, but it could not reveal the impact of their use within the institution. To get at this more elusive kind of topic, we relied on personal interviews and correspondence. Beginning in the summer of 1963 we conducted 209 interviews at 33 colleges and universities and central governing boards in 16 states. These are the institutions included in the interview sample:

University of California at Berkeley
University of California at Los Angeles
University of California Statewide
University of Colorado

Florida Board of Control of Higher Education
Florida State University
University of South Florida
University of Massachusetts
University of Michigan
Wayne State University
Michigan State University
Council of State College Presidents (Michigan)
Illinois State Board of Higher Education
Northern Illinois University
University of Illinois
Indiana University
Purdue University
University of Maryland
University of Minnesota
New Mexico State Board of Educational Finance
New Mexico State University
University of New Mexico
State University of New York at Buffalo
University of Oregon
University of Rhode Island
Texas Commission on Higher Education
University of Texas
University of Houston
University of Washington
American Council on Education (Washington, D.C.)
Coordinating Committee for Higher Education (Wisconsin)
Wisconsin State College Board of Trustees
University of Wisconsin

We selected these particular institutions for a variety of reasons. We wanted a representative distribution of institutions as far as size and region are concerned. We were also anxious to visit schools where especially interesting developments at the frontiers of managerial change were reported to us. We therefore went to New Mexico State University primarily because an institutional research director there was pioneering in administrative "games" and computer simulation. We went to Purdue because of its advanced work in computer scheduling of classrooms. We paid return visits to some institutions in order to observe changes in administrative practice—and reactions to that practice—over a period of time. One author did most of the interviewing in the eastern half of the country, while the other worked mainly in the midwestern and western states. Each made occasional sorties into the other's territory.

Most of the interviews were with university administrators, but we tried to talk also to faculty members and in a few cases to students. Along with our interviews on campus we profited substantially from conversations with academic officials at several regional and national meetings. At seminars sponsored by such groups as the Western Interstate Commission for Higher Education and the New England Board of Higher Education we obtained many valuable suggestions on where to go and what to look for. We also discovered that a university administrator is sometimes more disposed to talk candidly when he is away from his own desk.

As a matter of fact, the people we interviewed were remarkably forthright in their answers to our questions. The problem encountered in interviewing at institutions of higher education is not so much the reluctance of officials to talk, as it is that the meaning and direction of change on their own campus is often as confusing for university administrators as it is for outsiders. As standing practice we employed a uniform schedule of questions in our interviews, but in many cases the complexity and diversity of academic practice caused us to depart from this schedule during a large part of each interview.

Ordinarily we made notes during or immediately after interviews and then transcribed them more fully when we returned to our offices. In addition we usually prepared a summary analysis of our visit to each campus. This was helpful to the research partner who had not made the visit, since it is not always easy to put an interview report into proper perspective without the advantage of having been on the scene.

The questionnaire processing and the interviewing proceeded simultaneously. We tried as much as possible to make comparisons between findings in the two approaches, and there was no case in which our interviews contradicted the quantitative data generated by the questionnaire. Finally, as an additional check on the accuracy of our analysis, we sent copies of each of the major sections of our manuscript to a number of informed observers of these new developments in higher education for review.

Appendix B

THE QUESTIONNAIRE: A STATISTICAL ANALYSIS

I. The Questionnaire and the Response Population

Section I. Institutional Research

A. Is there an office or person specifically designated to carry on institutional research on your campus?

Yes ☐ If yes, please have the head of such an office or person complete Part B.

No ☐ If no, please return this section of the questionnaire to the address above.

B. These Items Are Directed to the Head of the Office or Person Designated To Carry On Institutional Research.

1. What is the official title or name of your office or position?
2. When was it first established? Date
3. Is institutional research carried on by other agencies in the university? Yes ☐ No ☐ If so, please identify names of other agencies and types of research responsibilities.

3a. If there are various agencies by which institutional research is carried on at your campus, does this suggest a need for better co-ordination of institutional research? Yes ☐ No ☐ Comment

4. How many professional staff employees does your agency employ?
5. How many graduate assistants does your agency utilize? ☐
6. What is the subject matter area of your own professional training or background, e.g., accounting, psychology, statistics?
7. Do you have an advanced degree? Yes☐ No ☐

7a. Please specify the degree you hold. M.A. or M.S. ☐ Ph.D. ☐ Other ☐ Please specify

8. What are the principal areas of training or backgrounds of the members of your professional staff?
9. Would you describe the work of your agency as being primarily oriented toward (please rank the areas below in the order of their importance to your office)
   - ☐ financial studies; e.g., cost analysis, etc.
   - ☐ faculty studies; e.g., faculty turnover, the effectiveness of teaching, etc.
   - ☐ student studies; e.g., drop-outs, etc.
   - ☐ other (please specify)

10. Does your agency have a faculty advisory committee? Yes □ No □
10a. If so, what is the major function or role of this committee?
11. To what officer in the university does your agency report?
12. Do you regard the office of institutional research on your campus as an arm of
    □ the administration.
    □ the faculty.
    □ neither (please specify, if necessary).
13. What is your policy regarding the distribution of your studies to members of the administration, faculty, and general public—e.g., is the circulation of some studies restricted to administrative officials only? Comment
14. Do you feel that the findings resulting from some of the studies conducted by your agency (e.g., cost data on certain areas of high-cost instruction) might cause major controversy if they were distributed to the general public or the state legislature?
    Yes □ No □ Comment
15. Some people look upon an office of institutional research as engaged primarily in basic fact-gathering operations. Others feel that such an agency plays an important role in making major university decisions. What do you regard as the major function of your office?
    □ basic data-gathering agency
    □ participant in major university decisions
    Comment
16. What, if any, major steps or changes in the university's policy or development in recent years have directly resulted from the work of the office of institutional research?
17. Does your agency conduct studies upon its own initiative, or are the studies it conducts usually assigned to it by the administration?
18. Is there a central co-ordinating body in your state which conducts institutional research?
    Yes □ No □ Comment
18a. If so, is the legislature showing an increasing tendency to look to such a co-ordinating body for basic data on the performance of individual institutions?
    Yes □ No □ Comment
19. It has been suggested by one authority that the institutional research director should be a university president's "right-hand man." Would you agree □ or disagree □? Comment
20. In your opinion, should the institutional research director
    a. □ make policy recommendations to university executives along with his reports.
    b. □ let his findings speak for themselves.

Comment

21. In brief, how would you summarize the role of institutional research at your university?

Name of official answering Section I

Name of institution

Section II. Electronic Data Processing

A. Does your institution employ electronic computers (as distinguished from older machine tabulating equipment) for administrative purposes within the institution?

Yes ☐ If the answer is yes, please complete the remaining portion of Section II.

No ☐ If the answer is no, please return this section of the questionnaire to the address above.

B. These Items Are Directed to the Heads of the Offices with Responsibility for the Operation of Electronic Computers for Administrative Purposes.

1. Is there a central agency in your institution specifically designated to operate computers which are used for administrative purposes?
   Yes ☐ No ☐
   If the answer is yes
   a. What is the name of the office (e.g., Data Processing Service)?
   b. To what university officer or committee is this office responsible?
   c. What kind and brand of computer equipment is used by this office?
   If the answer is no, or if additional offices operate computers,
   d. What offices *other than* a central computer facility operate computers for administrative purposes in your institution?
   e. What kind and brand of computer equipment is used by these offices?

2. Please check the administrative activities which presently involve the use of electronic computers. Please mark an "F" in the box if you plan to use computers in the future for this activity.
   a. Student Affairs
      ☐ 1) Admissions
      ☐ 2) Registration
      ☐ 3) Grading records
      ☐ 4) General student records
      ☐ 5) Other (please specify)
   b. Physical Plant Management
      ☐ 1) Space inventories
      ☐ 2) Space cost analysis
      ☐ 3) Assignment of classroom space
      ☐ 4) Assignment of office space
      ☐ 5) Other (please specify)
   c. Financial Administration
      ☐ 1) General accounting
      ☐ 2) Payroll
      ☐ 3) General inventories
      ☐ 4) Budget preparation
      ☐ 5) Cost analysis of operations
      ☐ 6) Investment records and analysis
      ☐ 7) Other (please specify)
   d. Policy Planning
      ☐ 1) Long-range planning
      ☐ 2) Institutional research
      ☐ 3) Simulation of institutional operations using statistical models
      ☐ 4) Other (please specify)

3. Using the figures 1, 2, 3, and 4, how would you numerically rank the four categories in question two in terms of the time they consume on computers at your institution?
   - ☐ a. Student Affairs
   - ☐ b. Physical Plant Management
   - ☐ c. Financial Administration
   - ☐ d. Policy Planning
   - ☐ e. Other (please specify)
4. We would be particularly interested in knowing more about your institution's use of computers for the simulation of campus operations, heuristic problem solving, or other forms of advanced computer analysis. If you are not using computers for such purposes now, do you have plans for such use in the future? Please comment below on any work or plans now in progress.
5. Some officials have been charged with "dehumanizing" their university because they have employed computers for admissions, registration, or other administrative activities. Have you encountered similar attitudes at your institution?
   Yes ☐ No ☐ Please comment.
6. Have you calculated unit costs for any of your computer operations?
   Yes ☐ No ☐ If so, please specify.

Name of official answering Section II
Name of institution

Section III. Budgeting
These Items Are Directed to the Office or Persons Responsible for the Preparation of the General Budget of Your Institution.

1. How would you describe the type of budget used by your institution? (We would appreciate receiving a copy of your current budget if one is available.)
   - ☐ a. Strictly an object budget, which is organized by objects of expenditure such as salaries, equipment, and postage.
   - ☐ b. A program budget, which is organized in categories which reflect the costs of fulfilling the principal functions or purposes of the institution, such as instruction, research, and extension service.
   - ☐ c. A mixture of object and program categories. If you check this one, please comment on the nature of the categories in the space below.
   - ☐ d. Other. Please describe your budget structure in the space below.
2. Does your institution have a specialized budget office?
   Yes ☐ No ☐
   If the answer is yes,
   a. What is the name of the office?
   b. To what officer or committee is the office responsible?
   c. How many professional staff members does this office employ? ☐
   d. How many graduate students does your agency utilize? ☐
   If the answer is no,
   e. What office has responsibility for the preparation of the budget?
3. Have changes in the method of budgeting occurred in the last decade?
   Yes ☐ No ☐ If the answer is yes, please specify in the space below.
4. Please check the items below for which quantitative formulas are used in

the preparation of the budget. (Space planning and utilization are covered in Section IV.)

☐ a. Student-faculty ratio
☐ b. The distribution of students between lower, upper, and graduate divisions
☐ c. Staffing formulas for faculty
☐ d. Staffing formulas for nonacademic personnel
☐ e. Other (please specify)

5. What areas of activity in your institution are subject to quantitative cost analysis (in which unit costs of operations are determined)? (Space planning and utilization are covered in Section IV.)
☐ a. Admissions (e.g., the unit cost of processing a single admission)
☐ b. Registration
☐ c. Payroll (e.g., unit cost of processing a salary check)
☐ d. Instructional costs (e.g., costs per student credit-hour)
☐ e. Costs of central services such as motor pool, food service
☐ f. Other (please specify)
6. Do you plan to institute any major revisions in your budgeting procedures in the near future? Yes ☐ No ☐ If so, please comment in the space below.

Name of official answering Section III
Name of institution

Section IV. Space Planning and Utilization
These Items Are Directed to the Office or Persons Responsible for the Planning and Utilization of Physical Space on Your Campus.

1. Does your institution have a specialized space-planning or space utilization office or official?
Yes ☐ No ☐
If the answer is yes
a. What is the name or title of the office or official?
b. To what university officer or committee is the office responsible?
c. How many professional staff members does the office employ? ☐
d. How many graduate students does your agency utilize? ☐
If the answer is no
e. What university office has responsibility for the planning and utilization of campus space?
2. Have changes in the methods of planning and assigning space occured in the last decade? Yes ☐ No ☐ If so, please comment below.
3. Please check the items for which formulas are used in the planning and utilization of campus space.
☐ a. Determining size of classroom in campus planning
☐ b. Assignment of classroom space
☐ c. Determining size of faculty offices in campus planning
☐ d. Assignment of faculty offices
☐ e. Determining size of student residence facilities
☐ f. Assignment of students to residences
☐ g. Long-range planning of building needs
☐ h. Other (please specify)
4. What areas of activity in your space program are subject to quantitative cost analysis?

- ☐ a. Costs of classroom space (e.g., x dollars per student station)
- ☐ b. Costs of office space
- ☐ c. Costs of student residence space
- ☐ d. Maintenance costs
- ☐ e. Development and planning costs
- ☐ f. Other (please specify)

5. Do you plan to institute any major revisions in your space management procedures in the near future? Yes ☐ No ☐ If so, please comment in the space below.

Name of official answering Section IV
Name of institution

TABLE B–1: REGIONAL CLASSIFICATION OF STATE-SUPPORTED FOUR-YEAR INSTITUTIONS OF HIGHER EDUCATION[a]

Northeast		South	
Connecticut	New York	Alabama	Mississippi
Maine	Pennsylvania	Arkansas	North Carolina
Massachusetts	Rhode Island	Delaware	Oklahoma
New Hampshire	Vermont	Florida	South Carolina
New Jersey		Georgia	Tennessee
		Kentucky	Texas
		Louisiana	Virginia
		Maryland	West Virginia
North Central		**West**	
Illinois	Missouri	Alaska	Montana
Indiana	Nebraska	Arizona	Nevada
Iowa	North Dakota	California	New Mexico
Kansas	Ohio	Colorado	Oregon
Michigan	South Dakota	Hawaii	Utah
Minnesota	Wisconsin	Idaho	Washington
			Wyoming

[a] We have employed throughout this study the regional divisions used by the U.S. Bureau of the Census.

TABLE B-2: RESPONSE POPULATION BY ENROLLMENT CLASS AND REGION

Enrollment	NE	%[a]	NC	%	S	%	W	%	Total	%
Under 2,000	23	24.0	15	15.6	41	42.7	17	17.7	96	100.0
2–10,000	27	18.2	36	24.4	59	39.8	26	17.6	148	100.0
Over 10,000	4	8.7	18	39.1	12	26.1	12	26.1	46	100.0
Total	54	18.6	69	23.8	112	38.6	55	19.0	290	100.0

	Under 2,000	%	2–10,000	%	Over 10,000	%	Total	%
NE	23	42.6	27	50.0	4	7.4	54	100.0
NC	15	22.0	36	52.0	18	26.0	69	100.0
S	41	37.0	59	53.0	12	10.0	112	100.0
W	17	31.0	26	47.0	12	22.0	55	100.0
Total	96	33.0	148	51.0	46	16.0	290	100.0

[a] Percentages are based on horizontal row totals.

II. Institutional Research

TABLE B-3: THE DISTRIBUTION OF INSTITUTIONAL RESEARCH OFFICES BY ENROLLMENT AND REGION

Fractions[a] of schools responding affirmatively to Question I.A.: Is there an office or person specifically designated to carry on institutional research on your campus? (Schools which did not respond are excluded.)

	Enrollment			
Region	Under 2,000	2–10,000	Over 10,000	Total
NE	3/23 (13%)	15/26 (53%)	2/4 (50%)	20/53 (37.7%)
NC	3/13 (23%)	14/35 (40%)	11/17 (65%)	28/65 (43%)
S	6/40 (15%)	25/55 (45.5%)	8/12 (67%)	39/107 (36.4%)
W	7/15 (46.5%)	19/23 (82.6%)	11/11 (100%)	37/49 (75.5%)
Total	19/91 (20.8%)	73/139 (52.5%)	32/44 (72.7%)	124/274 (45.2%)

[a] The numerator of each fraction is the number of schools responding affirmatively. The denominator is the total number of schools which responded to this question in a particular region and enrollment class.

TABLE B–4: THE CONCERNS OF INSTITUTIONAL RESEARCH; MAJOR ACTIVITIES AS RANKED IN IMPORTANCE BY IR DIRECTORS

Activity	1	%[a]	2	%	3	%	4	%	Total	%
Student studies	49	40	11	9	12	10	11	9	83	68
Faculty studies	29	23	28	23	19	15	5	4	81	65
Financial studies	21	17	16	13	19	15	11	9	67	54
Physical planning	15	12	0	0	4	3	3	2	22	17

[a] All percentage figures in this table are computed on a base of 124 state colleges and universities which responded affirmatively to our question regarding the existence of a specialized IR office at their institution.

TABLE B–5: INSTITUTIONAL RESEARCH AGENCIES: SIZE OF PROFESSIONAL STAFF

No. of Professional Employees	No. of Agencies	% (n = 124)
1	67	54.0
2	25	20.0
3	10	8.0
4	8	6.5
5	2	1.5
6	4	3.25
7	1	1.0
8 or more	2	1.5
Other[a]	5	4.25
Total	124	100.0

[a] This category includes institutions which did not answer this item as well as responses which were not classifiable.

III. Electronic Data Processing

TABLE B–6: THE DISTRIBUTION OF THE USE OF COMPUTERS FOR ADMINISTRATIVE PURPOSES

Fractions of schools responding affirmatively to Question II.A: Does your institution employ electronic computers for administrative purposes within the institution? (Schools not responding are excluded.)

	Enrollment			
Region	Under 2,000	2–10,000	Over 10,000	Total
NE	6/21 (28.6%)	10/27 (37%)	4/4 (100%)	20/52 (38.4%)
NC	2/13 (15.4%)	23/36 (64%)	17/17 (100%)	42/66 (63.5%)
S	10/37 (27%)	32/53 (60.5%)	11/12 (91.6%)	53/102 (52%)
W	2/14 (14.3%)	18/21 (85.7%)	8/11 (72.7%)	28/46 (60.9%)
Total	20/85 (23.5%)	83/137 (60.5%)	40/44 (91%)	143/266 (53.7%)

TABLE B–7: NUMBER AND PERCENTAGE OF INSTITUTIONS USING ELECTRONIC COMPUTERS FOR ADMINISTRATIVE PURPOSES WITHIN THE INSTITUTION

	Number	%
Yes	143	53
No	123	47
Total	266	100

	Number	%
Central agency	130[a]	91
No Central agency	13	9
Total	143	100

[a] The base numbers 143 and 130, as used in the following tables, differ slightly from the base of 134 employed in Chapter Two, but the ratios are virtually identical.

TABLE B–8: USE MADE OF COMPUTERS BY MAJOR ADMINISTRATIVE ACTIVITY ACCORDING TO TIME CONSUMED

Area of Administrative Concern	No. of Schools Ranking: 1st	2d	3d	4th	Total
Student affairs	89	44	3	0	136
Financial administration	47	56	10	7	120
Physical plant management	0	8	39	18	65
Policy planning	0	9	28	23	60
Total	136	117	80	48	381

TABLE B–9: HAVE YOU ENCOUNTERED CHARGES OF "DEHUMANIZING" UNIVERSITY OPERATIONS BY USING COMPUTERS?

	Number	%[a]
Yes	34	24
Limited	3	2
No	97	68
No response	9	6
Total	143	100

[a] Percentages based on 143 schools which indicated use of computers for administrative purposes.

TABLE B–10: ARE YOU NOW USING, OR DO YOU PLAN IN THE FUTURE TO USE COMPUTERS FOR THE SIMULATION OF CAMPUS OPERATIONS, HEURISTIC PROBLEM SOLVING, OR OTHER FORMS OF ADVANCED COMPUTER ANALYSIS?

	Number	%[a]
Not at present	53	37
Plans in progress	11	8
Yes	2	1
No response	77	54
Total	143	100

[a] Percentages based on 143 schools which indicated use of computers for administrative purposes.

TABLE B–11: IF THERE IS A CENTRAL COMPUTER AGENCY, TO WHAT UNIVERSITY OFFICER OR COMMITTEE IS THIS OFFICE RESPONSIBLE?

		Number	%[a]
	Financial administrator (e.g., business mgr., treasurer, VP for finance)	48	37
Nonfinancial top administrator	Academic administrator (e.g., academic dean, dean of the faculty or college, VP for academic affairs)	18	13.8
	President's office (Pres. or ass't.)	9	6.9
	Administrative dean or Administrative vice-president	9	6.9
	Registrar	9	6.9
	Research director	6	4.6
	Computer center committee	5	3.8
	Central state office	5	3.8
	Director independent lab (e.g., Agricultural Experiment Station)	5	3.8
	Director of admissions	4	3.1
	Math department	3	2.3
	None	1	.8
	Other	8	6.1
	Total	130	99.8

[a] Percentages based on 130 schools which indicated the existence of a central computer agency. Percentages total less than 100 because of rounding.

TABLE B–12: IF THERE IS NO CENTRAL COMPUTER AGENCY, WHAT OTHER OFFICES OPERATE COMPUTERS FOR ADMINISTRATIVE PURPOSES IN YOUR INSTITUTION?

	Number[a]	%
Computing facility	5	25
Registrar	4	20
Financial (e.g., comptroller, business office)	3	15
Admissions office	3	15
Dean of instruction	1	5
Research lab	1	5
Personnel	1	5
Space utilization	1	5
Math department	1	5
Total	20	100

[a] If there is no central agency, several offices in the same institution may operate computers.

TABLE B–13: HAVE YOU CALCULATED UNIT COSTS FOR COMPUTER OPERATIONS?

	Number	%[a]
Yes	19	13
In process	1	1
No	114	80
No response	9	6
Total	143	100

[a] Percentages based on 143 schools which indicated use of computers for administrative purposes.

IV. Budgeting

TABLE B–14: THE DISTRIBUTION OF SPECIALIZED BUDGET OFFICES BY ENROLLMENT AND REGION

Fractions of schools responding affirmatively to Question III.2: Does your institution have a specialized budget office? (Schools which did not respond are excluded.)

	Enrollment			
Region	Under 2,000	2–10,000	Over 10,000	Total
NE	0/19 (0%)	2/22 (9.1%)	4/4 (100%)	6/45 (13.3%)
NC	2/12 (16.7%)	5/34 (14.7%)	4/16 (25%)	11/62 (17.7%)
S	5/34 (14.7%)	11/50 (22%)	6/12 (50%)	22/96 (22.9%)
W	2/12 (16.7%)	5/23 (21.8%)	7/11 (63.6%)	14/46 (30.4%)
Total	9/77 (11.7%)	23/129 (17.8%)	21/43 (48.8%)	53/249 (21.3%)

TABLE B–15: TYPES OF BUDGETS

	No. of Schools	%
Object	63	24
Program	55	21
Mixture	141	55
Total	259	100

TABLE B–16: TO WHAT OFFICER OR COMMITTEE IS THE BUDGET OFFICE RESPONSIBLE?

	Number	%[a]
President	20	37.8
Financial administrator (e.g., comptroller, VP for business, business mgr., dean of finance)	27	51.0
Administrative dean or executive VP	3	5.7
Academic administrator (e.g., dean of the college, VP for academic affairs)	1	1.8
Other	2	3.7
Total	53	100.0

[a] Percentages based on 53 schools indicating the existence of a specialized budget office.

TABLE B–17: HOW MANY PROFESSIONAL STAFF MEMBERS DOES THIS OFFICE EMPLOY?

	Number	%[a]
0	1	1.9
1	12	22.6
2	16	30.2
3	8	15.1
4	3	5.7
5	1	1.9
6	2	3.8
7 or more	6	11.3
No response	4	7.6
Total	53	100.1

[a] Percentages based on 53 schools indicating the existence of a specialized budget office.

TABLE B–18: IF THERE S NO SPECIALIZED BUDGET OFFICE, WHAT OFFICE IS RESPONSIBLE FOR THE PREPARATION OF THE BUDGET?

	Number	%[a]
Business office	73	37.2
Comptroller	21	10.7
President	18	9.2
Vice-president	12	6.1
Dean	4	2.0
Other or no response	68	34.8
Total	196	100.0

[a] Percentages based on 196 schools which indicated they had no specialized budget office.

V. Space Utilization

TABLE B–19: THE DISTRIBUTION OF SPACE UTILIZATION OFFICES BY ENROLLMENT AND REGION

Fractions of schools responding affirmatively to Question IV.1: Does your institution have a specialized space planning or space utilization office or official?

	Enrollment			
Region	Under 2,000	2–10,000	Over 10,000	Total
NE	4/20 (20%)	15/26 (57.6%)	3/4 (75.0%)	22/50 (44.0%)
NC	2/11 (18.2%)	11/34 (32.2%)	12/15 (80.0%)	25/60 (41.6%)
S	1/37 (2.7%)	10/47 (21.3%)	7/12 (58.4%)	18/96 (18.7%)
W	3/13 (23.1%)	18/23 (78.3%)	8/10 (80.0%)	29/46 (63.0%)
Total	10/81 (12.3%)	54/130 (41.5%)	30/41 (73.2%)	94/252 (37.3%)

TABLE B–20: IF THERE IS A SPECIALIZED SPACE UTILIZATION OFFICE, TO WHAT UNIVERSITY OFFICER OR COMMITTEE IS THE OFFICE RESPONSIBLE?

	Number	%[a]
President	52	55.3
Vice-president	17	18.1
Executive dean	8	8.5
Space utilization or campus development committee	7	7.4
Planning office	3	3.2
Institutional research office	2	2.1
Other	3	3.2
No response	2	2.1
Total	94	99.9

[a] Percentages based on 94 schools which indicated the existence of a specialized space utilization office.

TABLE B–21: HOW MANY PROFESSIONAL STAFF MEMBERS DOES THE OFFICE EMPLOY?

	Number	%[a]
0	6	6.4
1	39	41.5
2	15	16.0
3	10	10.6
4	3	3.2
5	5	5.3
More than 5	5	5.3
No response	11	11.7
Total	94	100.0

[a] Percentages based on 94 schools which indicated the existence of a specialized space utilization office.

TABLE B–22: AREAS OF SPACE PROGRAM SUBJECTED TO COST ANALYSIS

Area	No. of Schools	%[a]
Cost of student residence space	119	47.2
Maintenance cost	108	42.8
Cost of classroom space	84	33.3
Cost of office space	64	25.4
Development and planning	50	19.8

[a] Based on 252 schools.

TABLE B–23: IF THERE IS NO SPECIALIZED SPACE UTILIZATION OFFICE, WHAT UNIVERSITY OFFICE HAS RESPONSIBILITY FOR THE PLANNING AND UTILIZATION OF CAMPUS SPACE?

	Number	%[a]
President's office	27	17.1
Dean	18	11.4
Registrar	11	7.0
Business office	10	6.3
Vice-president	9	5.7
Space committee	6	3.8
Buildings and grounds	4	2.5
Institutional research	3	1.9
No response or other	66	44.3
Total	154	100.0

[a] Percentages based on 154 schools which indicated they have no specialized space utilization office.

VI. Tests of Association

We applied statistical tests to a number of hypotheses about administrative practices identified in the questionnaire. We tested to see if the existence of a certain practice or office was associated with the size or region of an institution. In other tests we tried to find out if one administrative practice (e.g., computer use) was significantly associated with another practice (e.g., the use of quantitative formulas in budgeting). Finally, we tested for associations between different specialized offices within institutions. In these tests we employed the chi-square test with the Yates correction. The size and enrollment distribution of institutions that did not respond to the questionnaire were nearly the same as the distribution of the responding institutions, which made this test appropriate. We also took precautions to prevent distortions resulting from regional variations in the distribution of institutions according to size.

In each case we tested the null hypothesis that no association existed. After each statement is listed the degree of probability that the null hypothesis was true. If the probability that the association could have occurred by chance was less than .05 [P(Ho) < .05], the null hypotheses were rejected and the statements below were considered *confirmed.* If the probability was between .05 and .2, the outcome was considered *ambiguous.* If the probability was greater than .2, the null hypotheses were retained and the statements were *not confirmed.*

Generally speaking, large institutions are much more likely to employ new management practices than are small institutions. There are also significant regional variations, with the West clearly ahead of other regions in the innovation of techniques. But the tests of association among selected administrative practices gave us highly ambiguous results. Here, in summary form, are the propositions and the results of their test.

1. Large institutions are more likely to have offices of institutional research than smaller institutions. *Confirmed.* Less than one-fourth of the institutions under 2,000 have IR offices, while nearly three-fourths of the schools over 10,000 have them. P(Ho) < .001.

2. The existence of an office of institutional research is associated with the regional location of the institution. *Confirmed.* The South and Northeast have an extremely low incidence of such offices. The North Central region is about average. The West has a very high incidence. P(Ho) < .001.

3. Large institutions are more likely to use computers for administrative purposes than are smaller institutions. *Confirmed.* Slightly over one-fifth of the schools under 2,000 use computers, while over 90 per cent of schools with more than 10,000 students do so. P(Ho) < .001.

4. The use of computers for administrative purposes is associated with the regional location of the institution. *Ambiguous.* The West and North Central regions are above average in computer use, while the Northeast and South are below average. There is less than a 10 per cent probability that some sort of regional association does not exist. P(Ho) < .10.

5. Large institutions are more likely to have specialized budget offices than are smaller institutions. *Confirmed.* P(Ho) < .001.

6. The existence of a specialized budget office is associated with the regional location of the institution. *Not confirmed.* P(Ho) > .20.

7. Large institutions are more likely to have specialized space utilization offices than are smaller institutions. *Confirmed.* P(Ho) < .001.

8. The existence of a specialized space utilization office is associated with the regional location of the institution. *Confirmed.* Again, the West is the clear leader. P(Ho)<.001.

9. There is an association between the use of computers for administrative purposes and the use of quantitative formulas in budgeting. *Not confirmed.* P(Ho)>.30.

10. There is an association between the use of computers for administrative purposes and the use of quantitative formulas for space utilization. *Not confirmed.* P(Ho)>.30.

11. There is an association between the use of computers for administrative purposes and the use of quantitative cost analysis techniques in budgeting. *Ambiguous.* In spite of the high probability, this hypothesis was not regarded as confirmed because one region, the Northeast, shows a high association, while others show insignificant or negative relationships. P(Ho)<.01.

12. There is an association between the use of computers for administrative purposes and the use of quantitative cost analysis in space utilization. *Ambiguous.* In spite of the high probability, this hypothesis was not regarded as confirmed because one region, the South, distorted the national pattern. P(Ho)<.02.

13. Schools that use quantitative formulas in budgeting also tend to use them in space utilization. *Not confirmed.* P(Ho)>.30.

14. Schools that use quantitative cost analysis in budgeting also tend to use it in space utilization. *Ambiguous.* (PHo)<.20.

15. Schools that use computers for budget preparation or cost analysis tend to use quantitative formulas in budgeting. *Not confirmed.* P(Ho)>.90.

16. Schools that use computers for budget preparation or cost analysis also use quantitative cost analysis techniques in budgeting. *Ambiguous.* P(Ho)<.075.

VII. Mobility and Background of State College and University Presidents

The material in this section is based on a biographical analysis of the presidents of all four-year state-supported institutions of higher education. It was not a part of our regular questionnaire. The data were compiled from *Who's Who* for 1964–65.

We were interested in discovering whether the managerial revolution in higher education has been accompanied by any tendency to recruit university presidents from government or private industry rather than an educational background. We found no evidence to support this view. The president of an academic institution is most likely to have been promoted to his present post from a background in university government, particularly on the academic side. The evidence further suggests a strong inclination on the part of larger universities to select their presidents from among incumbents at other institutions.

Also significant are the data suggesting that the president of a smaller institution is considerably more likely to be a native of his school's region or state than is the head of a larger college. In this connection it is interesting to note the very high mobility in presidential selection evidenced in the West, and the comparatively low mobility displayed in the South.

TABLE B–24: PERCENTAGE OF STATE INSTITUTIONS WHOSE PRESIDENT IS NATIVE TO THEIR REGION

Region	Under 2,000	2,000–10,000	Over 10,000	Total
NE	16/21 (76%)	19/34 (56%)	4/6 (67%)	39/61[a] (64%)
NC	8/10 (80%)	29/39 (74%)	12/20 (60%)	49/69 (70%)
S	37/41 (90%)	56/66 (85%)	15/18 (83%)	108/125 (86%)
W	4/13 (31%)	9/29 (31%)	6/17 (35%)	19/59 (32%)
Total	65/85 (76%)	113/168 (67%)	37/61 (61%)	215/314 (68%)

[a] The denominator of each fraction is the total number of schools in a particular region and enrollment class. The numerator is the number of schools in that category whose president is native to the region in which the school is located. Percentages are based on the fractions.

TABLE B–25: PERCENTAGE OF STATE INSTITUTIONS WHOSE PRESIDENT IS NATIVE TO THEIR STATE

Region	Under 2,000	2,000–10,000	Over 10,000	Total
NE	9/21 (43%)	13/34 (38%)	1/6 (17%)	23/61[a] (38%)
NC	4/10 (40%)	12/39 (31%)	5/20 (25%)	21/69 (30%)
S	25/41 (61%)	35/66 (53%)	10/18 (56%)	70/125 (56%)
W	3/13 (23%)	7/29 (24%)	2/17 (12%)	12/59 (20%)
Total	41/85 (48%)	67/168 (40%)	18/61 (30%)	126/314 (40%)

[a] The denominator of each fraction is the total number of schools in a particular region and enrollment class. The numerator is the number of schools in that category whose president is native to the region in which the school is located. Percentages are based on the fractions.

TABLE B–26: STATE COLLEGE AND UNIVERSITY PRESIDENTS: EARNED DEGREES AND FIELDS OF INTEREST

(percentages)

Field of Interest	Degrees		
	Ph.D.[b]	M.A.	B.A.
Total (n = 298)[a]	88	9	3
General Education	41	3	
History, law, politics	15	1	
English, Foreign languages	7		
Economics	4	1	
Chemistry	3		
Sociology	2		
Engineering	2		1
Agriculture	2	1	
Physics	2		
Psychology	1		
Philosophy	1		
Botany	1		
Mathematics	1		
Biology	1		
Medicine	1		
Business administration		1	
Other	3	2	2

[a] For 15 presidents no information as to field of interest was available.

[b] Includes Ed.D. In cases where the field in which the Ph.D. was earned was not indicated, the teaching background of the individual was taken as a basis for inclusion.

TABLE B–27: GENERAL AREAS OF EXPERIENCE OF STATE COLLEGE AND UNIVERSITY PRESIDENTS BY SIZE OF INSTITUTION

(percentages)

Occupation[a]	Under 2,000 (n = 84)	2,000–10,000 (n = 168)	Over 10,000 (n = 61)	Total Percentage of Presidents
(1) College teaching	77	76	85	79
(2) University gov't.				
a. Acad. admin.	57	69	75	67
b. Business admin.	14	17	20	17
c. Previous pres.	11	16	28	19
(3) State, local, federal education admin.	40	43	10	36
(4) Public service[b]	6	7	10	7
(5) Business, law, and journalism	1	2	7	3
(6) Professional military	4	—	—	1
(7) Politics	—	2	—	1

[a] For occupation categories (1), (2), and (3), a period of one year in the designated activities was considered sufficient for inclusion in our data. For categories (4) to (7), the basis for inclusion was (a) occupation immediately prior to assumption of present position or (b) a minimum of three consecutive years in the listed occupation. Item (6) was limited to career officers.

[b] This category includes local, state, or federal noneducation service, foundations, and other independent agency work, e.g., Carnegie Corporation, American Council on Education.

TABLE B–28: OCCUPATION OF STATE COLLEGE AND UNIVERSITY PRESIDENTS IMMEDIATELY PRIOR TO ASSUMPTION OF PRESENT POST BY ENROLLMENT CLASS OF INSTITUTION

(percentages)

Occupation	Under 2,000 (n = 84)	2,000–10,000 (n = 168)	Over 10,000 (n = 61)	Total Percentage of Presidents
(1) College teaching	23	10.5	10	14
(2) University gov't.				
a. Academic admin.	44	56	52	52
b. Business admin.	3	4	3	4
c. Previous pres.	13	12.5	23	15
(3) State, local, federal education admin.	12	15	2	11
(4) Public service	2	1	5	2
(5) Business, law and journalism	—	1	5	1
(6) Professional military	3	—	—	1
(7) Politics	—	—	—	—
	100.0	100.0	100.0	100.0

TABLE B–29: AVERAGE LENGTH OF SERVICE OF STATE COLLEGE AND UNIVERSITY PRESIDENTS, BY REGION

	NE	NC	S	W	Total
Years Length of Service	11.4	12.1	11.1	9.2	10.9

Appendix C

A COMPARATIVE STUDY OF UNIVERSITY ADMINISTRATION

In view of the extensive managerial changes that have occurred in American higher education, it would not be unnatural to expect that similar developments are taking place in other advanced societies. Different as the tradition and practice of higher education are in each country, universities throughout the world have been subject to the vast expansion in size which has triggered so much managerial innovation in the United States. However, the response to date does not indicate that institutions of higher learning abroad have seen anything like the degree of managerial change that has occurred in the United States. Some of the reasons for this difference in international experience are explored in this report.

UNIVERSITY EXPANSION ABROAD

Even a cursory glance at the statistics on higher education in European and Commonwealth countries reveals the striking increases in student enrollment which have taken place during the last fifteen years. As Table C–1 indicates, four of these countries—Australia, France, West Germany, and Sweden—more than doubled the number of students registered at their colleges and universities from 1949 to 1964. For the same period, large increases in student population were also reported by Canada (95 per cent), the Netherlands (83 percent), Italy (55 per cent), and Great Britian (49 per cent). By way of comparison, from 1949 to 1964 the total student population in American colleges and universities climbed 84 per cent.

This enrollment pressure upon European and Commonwealth systems of higher education is expected to continue through the remainder of the current decade and beyond. The report on higher education in Great Britain prepared by a committee headed by Lord Robbins warned that British universities would have to accommodate as many as 350,000 students by 1980.[1] Similar rates of increases in student enrollment may be expected in most of the remaining countries included in Table C–1.

Several factors account for this great expansion in university population in Europe and the Commonwealth. Most obvious perhaps is the sharp rise in the postwar birth rate. In recent years this phenomenon, accompanied in some countries by a relaxation of the strict rules governing admission and graduation practices in the secondary school system, has created a widening pool of univer-

[1] *Report of the Committee on Higher Education* (London: H.M. Stationery Office, 1963), p. 160. Hereafter this report will be referred to as the Robbins Report.

TABLE C–1: NUMBER OF STUDENTS IN UNIVERSITIES AND EQUIVALENT COLLEGES IN SELECTED EUROPEAN AND COMMONWEALTH COUNTRIES: 1949–70

(thousands)

	1949/50	1959/60	1963/64	1970/71
Great Britain	85	104	127	200
Australia	28	47	69	114
Canada	81	102	158	312
France	137	202	313	500
West Germany	102	200	263	400
Netherlands	29	37	53	59
Italy	146	176	226	—
Sweden	13	33	54	80
Switzerland	17	20	27	—
U.S.A.	2,457	3,402	4,529	7,000

SOURCE: See pp. 172–173.

sity-age students whose very presence exerts an increasing pressure upon the universities to expand. This pressure has been particularly acute in such countries as West Germany and France, where completion of the *Abitur* or *baccalauréat* has in the past automatically guaranteed a place in a university or other institution of higher learning.

In addition to this expansion in the absolute size of the age group eligible for entry into higher education abroad, there has also been a substantial growth in the percentage of university-age students seeking admission to institutions of higher education (see Table C–2).

A number of developments have contributed to the fact that so many more young people are now setting their sights on a university career. Rising standards of living, the increasing provision of public and private student grants and loans, the impressive new schemes for university housing, and the obvious intent of the governments concerned to make a determined effort to provide facilities for higher education have all served to stimulate educational aspirations on the part of the new generation.

Along with this increasing demand for advanced education on the part of university-age students, the expansion of the universities, particularly in the science and engineering faculties, also reflects the mounting need for well-trained administrators, technicians, engineers, and scientists in the booming economies of European and Commonwealth countries. The Robbins Committee, in recommending university status for British Colleges of Advanced Technology, urged Great Britian "to demonstrate beyond all doubt that it is prepared to give to technology the prominence that the economic needs of the future will surely demand."[2] The founding of technological colleges and universities in the Netherlands, Sweden, and New Zealand in recent years also serves to illustrate the growing concern of foreign governments over this vital area of education.

[2] The Robbins Report, p. 128.

TABLE C–2: PERCENTAGE OF UNIVERSITY-AGE STUDENTS ENTERING HIGHER EDUCATION IN SELECTED COUNTRIES: 1958/59 AND 1968/69

Selected Countries	Relevant Age	Size of Relevant Age Group (thousands)		Percentage in Higher Education	
		1958/59	1968/69	1958/59	1968/69
Great Britain	18	637	766	12	17
France	18	580	824	9	15
New Zealand	18	35	49	15	24
Sweden	20	94	128	11	18
U.S.A.	18	2,299	3,468	35	46

SOURCE: *Report of the Committee on Higher Education* (London: H.M. Stationery Office, 1963), Appendix Five, Table 1, p. 7, and Table 7, p. 11 (size of age group); Table 3, p. 9, and Table 9, p. 13 (percentage entering higher education). Hereafter this document will be referred to as the Robbins Report, Appendix Five.

The boom in student enrollments abroad has led to both an expansion of existing colleges and universities and the establishment of new institutions. One of the first effects of surging enrollments was a great increase in the size of existing institutions. Whereas in 1953 only 28 per cent of the students attending universities in the countries included in Table C–3 attended institutions of over 10,000 enrollment, by 1964 this figure had jumped to 57 per cent. Similarly, while in 1953 there were only six universities with student enrollments of 10,000 or more, by 1964 the number of such institutions had risen to thirty-five.

TABLE C–3: PERCENTAGE OF STUDENTS IN SELECTED EUROPEAN AND COMMONWEALTH COUNTRIES, BY SIZE OF UNIVERSITY (AND EQUIVALENT COLLEGES) ENROLLMENT: 1953/54 AND 1963/64

Selected countries	Size of Institution: Under 2,000		2,000 to 10,000		Over 10,000	
	53/54	63/64	53/54	63/64	53/54	63/64
Great Britain	16	8	61	73	23	19
Australia	11	7	89	36	—	57
France	1	—	58	16	41	84
West Germany	5	2	86	39	9	59
Italy	10	5	50	37	40	58
Netherlands	18	6	82	94	—	—
Sweden	36	8	64	25	—	67
Switzerland	24	8	76	92	—	—

SOURCE: See pp. 172–173.

Fewer than 5 per cent of the existing institutions have been founded since 1953. There are clear indications, however, that this proportion will rise as more and more universities reach the limits of expansion considered acceptable by a tradition-oriented academic community. Up to this point Great Britain leads all other countries in the establishment of new schools. Since 1950 it has founded seven new universities and granted university status to several Colleges of Advanced Technology. Australia,[3] France,[4] West Germany,[5] and the Netherlands[6] have also made significant efforts to set up new institutions, with the promise of even more impressive steps in this direction in the future.

Despite the apparent willingness of most European and Commonwealth countries to take the measures necessary to ensure an expanded system of higher education, the supply of university places and physical facilities, to say nothing of qualified academic personnel, has generally failed to keep up with demand. Student complaints against overcrowded classrooms, limited access to professors, insufficient or poor quality scientific equipment, and a general lack of personal attention on the part of university authorities are as prevalent in Europe and the Commonwealth as they are in the United States. France in recent years has witnessed a number of strikes by both students and teachers, "designed to call attention to the gross overcrowding in many centers and to the inadequate pace of capital investment and staff recruitment."[7]

In this rapidly changing environment, universities abroad have come under considerable pressure to adapt their organization and procedures to meet the new demands upon them. However, the extent to which such administrative adaption can occur in any organizational system is greatly affected by the structure and traditions of the institutions under stress. In the case of European universities, these traditions are the product of centuries of development, and they are highly resistant to change.

TRADITIONAL UNIVERSITY ADMINISTRATION

The traditional pattern of university administration in most European and Commonwealth countries, while varying in specific detail from country to country and from institution to institution, reveals a clear subordination of administration to academic influence. While such distinctly administrative officials as registrars, secretaries, bursars, and their various assistants have long been established and accepted features of most European and Commonwealth universities, their power and responsibilities have been far more narrowly restricted than is the case with university administrators in this country. The chief executive officer and his principal subordinates have tended, especially on the Continent, to view themselves as servants of the academic faculty rather than as powers in their own right.

Recent years have not brought any rapid change in this respect. Despite the fact that the size, cost, and complexity of university operations in Europe and

[3] The Robbins Report, Appendix Five, p. 31.

[4] *Ibid.*, pp. 73–74. See also *Education in France* (published by the Cultural Services of the French Embassy), No. 26 (December, 1964), pp. 15, 18.

[5] Walter Hahn, "Patterns and Trends in West German Universities," *Journal of Higher Education*, Vol. 36 (May, 1955), pp. 245–53.

[6] The Robbins Report, Appendix Five, p. 117.

[7] The Robbins Report, Appendix Five, p. 74.

the Commonwealth have continued to increase, there is little evidence to indicate that the administrative hierarchy in these institutions has come to occupy anything like the strong and often independent position of its American counterpart, described by one English observer as that "shadowy, powerful entity in American university life."[8]

There have, of course, been demands and suggestions for expanding the authority of the university administrator abroad. However, opposition to such proposals, coming primarily from well-entrenched academicians wary of any development which might pose a threat to their predominant influence, has remained both vociferous and highly effective. This section will explore some of the factors which have played an important role in limiting the influence of university administration in European and Commonwealth universities. Of chief importance in this respect have been the historically prestigious position of the academic hierarchy, the pervasive intervention of state ministries of education in the administration of institutions of higher education on the European continent, and the rather limited conception of university responsibility for student welfare which prevails in most institutions of higher education outside the United States.

The Predominance of the Academic Hierarchy.

Various historical considerations, including general acceptance, at least in theory, of the university as a "community of scholars" with the right to academic self-government, have been chiefly responsible for the strong position of the academic staff in European and Commonwealth universities. Organized into university senates, individual faculties and departments, the senior academicians have always controlled the highest policy-making bodies of their universities. While lay elements have also been present in these councils, and even numerically predominant in some, the views held by the faculty representatives have usually proved decisive.[9]

At the same time, of course, the faculty has been quite reluctant to extend this concept of faculty participation in university government to lower echelons of its own ranks. What academic self-government has meant essentially is rule by a small group of senior professors in every university. Often there is but one professorship or Chair in each field or department. The university senate and the governing organs of the various faculties and departments normally consist of all the full professors along with a few representatives drawn from the rest of the teaching staff.

Under this arrangement the professors not only have an important voice in the planning of academic policy, but they also play a continuing role in university administration as well. Many administrative functions which in American universities are carried on by a number of full-time officials, such as admissions and student discipline, have in other countries been placed within the range of responsibility of the faculty itself.

The chief means by which the faculty makes and enforces its decisions has been the committee system, at least in those cases (in the larger European and

[8] Elizabeth Sewell, "Flexibility in American Universities," *Universities Quarterly*, Vol. 13 (May, 1959), p. 280.

[9] See J. Blondel, "The State and the Universities," in Paul Halmos (ed.), *Sociological Studies in British University Education*, Monograph No. 7 of *The Sociological Review* (Keele: University of Keele, 1963), pp. 31–43.

Commonwealth universities, for example) where university and faculty governing bodies have been too large for effective conduct of university business. At the university level, committees which have been charged with distinctly academic functions, such as curriculum planning or admissions procedures, are usually restricted in membership to senior professors, with a few administrators included in an ex officio capacity. In those university-level committees where budget planning, space allocation, salary schedules, and similar questions having administrative implications are discussed, membership has often included high university officials and important lay personnel as well as academic representatives.

Participation in the work of these committees has long been regarded by the professorial staff as both a privilege and a duty. Overlapping membership on several committees has not been uncommon. It is in fact made necessary by the limited number of full professors available and the reluctance of these individuals to share power with either the rest of the teaching staff or the full-time university administrators. And as long as the size of universities remained limited, the pressures of committee work did not interfere with the ability of the senior academic to carry on his own scholarly activities.

The process of decision making in these faculty-dominated universities has been subject to sharp criticism from some quarters. In a discussion of British university government, G. E. Aylmer argues that the development of academic policy under this system often exhibits such characteristics as a "passion for secrecy . . . in the higher ranks," "log rolling," and "empire building."[10] Secrecy, Aylmer asserts, occurs "often over matters where it is patently ludicrous, e.g. university expansion in the mid-1960's, or over questions on which the university and the public have a reasonable right to be informed, e.g. departmental expenditure."[11] It has also been said that outside political connections, personal rivalries, and historical tradition play an important role in determining the final outcome of faculty debate over academic issues.

As a consequence of the dominant position of the academic staff in European and Commonwealth universities, only limited authority has been delegated to the chief executive officers of these institutions. It should be added, however, that there exist substantial differences in this regard between Commonwealth and Continental universities. Thus, the vice-chancellor or principal in Australia or Great Britain, by virtue of his much longer tenure and the greater freedom of his institution from state control, has held a much stronger position in the councils of his university than has the rector in the Italian, German, or French university.

The basic duties with which the chief executive officer is charged can range very widely. As is the case with the American university president, many of his duties center on external rather than internal affairs. He represents the university in its contacts with state ministries and other public organizations concerned with higher education and the universities. He must take an active role in the activities of such interuniversity organizations as the West German Rectors' Conference or the Committee of Vice-Chancellors and Principals in Great

[10] G. E. Aylmer, "University Government—But By Whom," *Universities Quarterly*, Vol. 13 (November, 1958), pp. 45–54.

[11] *Ibid.*, p. 47. See also the brief article on this subject by D. A. K. Black, "Intramural Communication," *Universities Quarterly*, Vol. 17 (June, 1963), pp. 271–73.

Britain.[12] As in the United States, although to a lesser extent, the chief executive officer is also obliged to keep in touch with potential donors and important political figures.

Despite the wide range of duties assigned to the chief executive officer, his power to effect real changes in the life of the university remains severely limited, particularly in Continental universities. For one thing, the selection of the chief executive officer is usually subject to approval in one form or another by the faculties at the university he is to govern. Ordinarily, he is a distinguished professor drawn from the teaching staff of the university, although there have been notable exceptions to this rule, particularly in Australia and Great Britain.[13] Under these circumstances it is highly unlikely that a chief executive will be selected who does not share in great part the traditional values and ambitions of the senior faculty, including the fear of state interference with the university and attachment to the principle of academic control over the affairs of the university.

The brevity of his tenure in office, which usually extends from one to three years, has been another important factor limiting the influence of the chief executive in European institutions. A short term of office not only discourages an ambitious university head from attempting to augment his own power, but it also limits long-range planning and hinders the development of proposals for university reform. Moreover, the small size of the rector's personal staff, in contrast to that of some American university presidents, has mirrored accurately the restricted scope and power of his office.

Among the many groups with which the chief executive shares power in performing his duties are deans, representatives of the state, individual faculty members, independent-minded subordinates in the administrative hierarchy, and a variety of powerful faculty and university committees. The precise nature of this division of power varies according to the institution, the country, and, as might be expected, the personality of the university head. But however these factors operate, rarely has a rector or a vice-chancellor made an important policy decision without formal consultation with the individuals and organizations most directly concerned, including, in some cases, the students.[14]

To assist the rector or vice-chancellor in reaching decisions which affect the university as a whole, there exists in most European and Commonwealth universities a formal executive committee. This body usually consists of the rector or vice-chancellor, his principal subordinates, the annually elected deans of the various academic faculties, other senior academicians, and, on occasion, representatives from state ministries or local interested authorities. Within this executive committee the position of the chief executive has usually been, at best, that of *primus inter pares*.

[12] The West German Rectors' Conference and the Committee of Vice-Chancellors and Principals in Great Britain are independent organizations of institutions of university status established to discuss problems in higher education in these countries. They have no statutory basis or executive power.

[13] For an interesting account of the difficulties faced by one Australian university vice-chancellor who came to his position from outside the teaching profession, see A. P. Rowe, *If The Gown Fits* (London: Cambridge University Press, 1960).

[14] In many British, Australian, and German universities there are elected student representatives sitting on the highest university bodies. Usually they are "silent" members, however.

In some German universities the authority of the rector has been further reduced by the practice of appointing "curators" to supervise the financial and other housekeeping activities of the institution. Thus, in the Prussian universities of Göttingen, Kiel, and Münster, the minister of education of the state "maintains an official who is designated as *Kurator* (executive officer of the governing board). This official is placed in charge of all the funds made available to the university by the ministry. He also manages the property belonging to the institution."[15] In recent years this pattern has been changing in the direction of giving university authorities the right to nominate the *Kurator* and to assume in general a greater role in the nonacademic administration of their institution.[16]

State Intervention in University Administration

Another reason for the lack of a well-developed administrative structure in a great many foreign universities is the fact that numerous administrative functions related to the operation of these institutions are carried on by various state agencies, most notably the ministries of education and finance. This has been particularly true in the case of universities on the European continent.[17] Thus in France the state has long held the legal right to determine university curricula, make appointments to teaching and administrative staffs, decide upon the allocation of university expenditures, and supervise, through its local representatives, the administrative affairs of institutions of higher education. Indeed, centralized control over universities can be so thorough that "a timetable, the purchasing of a calculating machine or the printing of a book all require Ministerial approval."[18] Elsewhere in western Europe the general fiscal and administrative position of the universities has not been much different, though state control over such basically academic matters as admissions, examinations, and course curricula has been much less common than in France.

As a result of this traditional pattern of state control over continental universities, decision-making authority in many areas has been placed in the hands of civil servants in the appropriate ministries and state agencies. Plans for university expansion on the European continent are largely prepared and implemented by civil servants, subject to the approval of the minister in charge and the parliament, which must vote the funds. The ministry of education also plays an important role in decisions to establish new professorial chairs, to raise academic salaries, or to construct additional classroom buildings. A great deal of administrative influence over academic affairs has thus been located at levels of government considerably removed from the university itself. The scope of government control over academic life is underlined in many European universities by the presence on campus of a number of state-appointed officials responsible for supervising the financial and general housekeeping affairs of institutions of higher learning.

To be sure, the extent of formal government control over the activities of Continental universities should not be exaggerated. In practice, the ministries

[15] Hahn, "Patterns and Trends in West German Universities," p. 249.

[16] *Ibid.*

[17] This pattern of state control does not prevail with respect to British universities, which have traditionally enjoyed a position of legal autonomy. However, as the discussion in the following section will show, this long-standing position of independence is presently undergoing some pressure for modification in Great Britain.

[18] The Robbins Report, Appendix Five, p. 67.

have been highly responsive to the opinions of the academic staff in the shaping of policies affecting higher education. The high prestige of the academic profession in most European countries has permitted it to exert a great deal of indirect influence on government policy in such vital areas as the appointment of staff, the determination of curricula, and the admission and examination of students. Moreover, even on issues involving substantial outlays of government funds, such as salary schedules or building construction, the academic staff, through a network of advisory committees, strategically placed sympathizers, and even seats in parliament, has been able to influence the final shape of policy. Thus in France, perhaps the most extreme case of ostensible government control over education, the director of higher education in the Ministry of National Education is usually a distinguished professor; senior faculty members "are able in practice to exercise considerable influence over the appointment and dismissal of members of their staff"; and the Conseil de l'Enseignement Superieure, described below, has played a decisive role in ministerial policy determination:

> The Conseil de l'Enseignement Superieure meets under the chairmanship of the director of higher education, but is largely composed of active academics. It deals with matters of university administration, discipline, curricula and examinations. Although in theory it is only advisory, it is in practice always consulted on major questions of policy and its advice is seldom ignored. The Conseil, although a large body in itself, works through a number of subcommittees; and at least ensures an approach to the type of academic participation in the making of decisions affecting the universities that is achieved in Great Britain through the University Grants Committee.[19]

Consequently it should come as no surprise that the battles which have periodically broken out in European countries over questions affecting higher education and the universities have generally reflected differences of opinion between two or more competing academic factions, rather than between faculty members on the one hand and government officials on the other. As a rule the sheer complexity of university operations, particularly on the academic side, compounded by the difficulty of obtaining reliable information on which to base policy decisions, has worked to reduce the real impact of government intervention in university affairs. In short, the role of the state has remained restricted. As Blondel has put it, "It accepts the advice which is given to it. . . . French universities are supervised by the Ministry; but the civil servants who are supervisors are surrounded and advised by numerous committees composed of academics."[20]

The Limited Role of the University

One of the most important factors contributing to the growth of university administration in the United States has been the willingness of institutions of higher education to provide students with a wide range of services quite apart from teaching itself. These nonacademic functions include the provision of housing, athletic, eating, and other physical facilities designed to enhance student welfare. The assumption by American universities of responsibility for

[19] *Ibid.*, p. 68. The Comite Consultatif des Universites plays a similar role with respect to staff appointments.

[20] Blondel, "The State and the Universities," p. 35.

these student services has required the establishment on university campuses of an elaborate administrative apparatus manned by numerous nonacademic officials.

In Europe, on the other hand, many of these nonacademic student needs are met, not by the university, but by outside groups, particularly student organizations. In Sweden, for example, student hostels are constructed and maintained by student organizations (with state and private financial assistance). In Germany and the Netherlands these organizations assist their members in finding housing, in making travel arrangements, and by providing some means of financial assistance to needy students. In France there are national agencies such as the Centre des Oeuvres Universitaires (responsible for student hostels) which also play an important role in removing responsibility for student welfare from the university itself.[21] In Great Britain student unions run restaurants, housing bureaus, employment agencies, and carry on "other forms of welfare work."[22]

The small scope of the residential facilities provided by universities for students eliminates the need for cadres of local administrative personnel to manage these units. In Australia, for example, only 14 per cent of all full-time students lived in university-associated hostels in 1963. In France the comparable figure was 12 per cent (1962), in West Germany 10 per cent (1962), in Sweden 10 per cent (1958), and in Great Britain 28 per cent (1962).[23]

Moreover, most European and Commonwealth institutions have not maintained the rather elaborate record-keeping system for students so common to American colleges and universities. Registration procedures have been comparatively simple and direct. Normally it is up to the student himself to keep his record up to date. The need for clerical personnel to maintain an accurate file on each student has also been reduced by the fact that the credit-hour system, a veritable bulwark of the American university, has been relatively unknown in the European academic environment. Finally, the curriculum of European universities has been quite simple as compared to the large array of courses, seminars, and other formal learning opportunities available to the average American student, and this also has trimmed the need for university administration.

Furthermore, once a student has graduated from a European university he is much less an object of concern as an alumnus than is the case in the United States. In large part this may be due to the fact that most universities in Europe and the Commonwealth have been largely or completely dependent upon the government for their income, and there has been little incentive until recent years for large-scale efforts to raise money from alumni or other outside sources. At one fell swoop this eliminates the need to administer either alumni relations or the development function.

In summary it is clear that the role of administrators at most universities abroad has remained considerably less developed than it is in this country, and where administration exists, it has been largely subservient to the faculty. In

[21] The Robbins Report, Appendix Five, p. 67. See the description of French student insurance programs, health services, and information bureaus in Anthony Kerr, *Universities of Europe* (Westminster, Eng.: The Canterbury Press, 1962), pp. 149–52.

[22] Kerr, *Universities of Europe*, p. 115.

[23] See the Robbins Report, Appendix Five: Australia, p. 37; France, p. 72; West Germany, p. 97; Sweden, p. 147. For Great Britain, see the Robbins Report, p. 194.

recent years, however, there have been several indications that the structure of many European and Commonwealth universities has been slowly changing under the pressure of increased enrollments and government grants.

PORTENTS OF CHANGE

In the face of the onrush of students and confronted with the need to train growing numbers of scientists, engineers, technicians, and administrators, governments in Europe and the Commonwealth over the last ten years have embarked on massive programs of financial assistance designed to help institutions of higher learning meet their new responsibilities. Inevitably, attention has been focused as well upon shortcomings in existing patterns of educational organization, for it has been recognized that university administration, as traditionally constituted, was not always adequate to handle the flow of either students or funds.

With a view to improving university administration, the governments of several countries, including France, the Netherlands, Sweden, and West Germany, have taken concrete steps to increase the power of the chief university executive. In France, for example, the authority of the *recteur* in such vital areas as budget preparation and curricula determination was "sizably" increased in 1962.[24] And in Holland, where it was the normal practice for the rectorship to change hands annually, the Higher Education Act of 1961 permitted rectors to hold office for as long as four years, thereby providing greater continuity and experience in this position.[25]

West Germany, with its provision for *Land* control over university administrative affairs, exhibits the same trend. Thus in the West German universities of Freiburg, Tübingen, Heidelberg, Bonn, and Marburg, the tasks of the state administration "are entrusted to the *Rektor* and are to be carried out on the basis of his directives and with the help of a chancellor subordinate to him.[26] The *Rektor* thereby achieves a prominent status as both head of the university's system of self-government and local representative of the *Land* ministry of education. A similar pattern has been proposed for the new university to be established at Regensburg, in Bavaria, with the added proviso that a committee composed of seven members of the teaching staff be created to advise the *Rektor* and his Chancellor. In the state of Hesse strong support has been given to a plan whereby university finances would be entrusted to a chancellor nominated by the senate and working under the direction of the *Rektor*. These reforms are mainly designed to strengthen the position of the *Rektor* vis-à-vis the state. But there have also been proposals to give the *Rektor* a stronger position within the framework of the academic community itself.[27] Moreover, the necessity of lengthening the *Rektor's* term of office appears to be widely recognized in West Germany.

In Great Britain and Australia, the committees appointed to study and make recommendations on higher education to the legislature reached the conclusion that the office of the vice-chancellor needed strengthening by the addition of

[24] Blondel, "The State and the Universities," p. 39.

[25] The Robbins Report, Appendix Five, pp. 107–8.

[26] Hahn, "Patterns and Trends in West German Universities, p. 249.

[27] *Ibid.*, pp. 249–52. See also Ralph Dahrendorf, "Die Faultaten und ihre Reform," *Hochschuldienst*, XVII (February 27, 1964), 1.

full-time staffs to assist in its work.[28] In the words of the British Committee on Higher Education, "there is a grave danger that the needs of expansion and the increasingly complex relations between institutions of higher education and government will impose upon the heads of universities a quite insupportable burden, unless steps are taken to relieve them. . . . No other enterprise would impose on its chairman the variety and burden of work that the modern university requires of its vice-chancellor. We recommend that governing bodies should give serious attention to improving their organization here."[29]

The Committee on Higher Education also proposed the "appointment of permanent pro-vice-chancellors" in certain institutions, while noting that "in others more complex measures involving the use of committees of senior academic and administrative staff may be thought to be the better arrangement."[30] At one point the committee went so far as to suggest that "in some cases both registry and finance departments would benefit from the advice of modern business consultants."[31]

Another proposal for the improvement of university administration in Great Britain has come from C. Northcote Parkinson, who has called for a "staff course in higher administration, to be supervised by retired Vice-Chancellors and held at some center for research which could be furnished with all the information obtainable about all the universities of the world."[32] He suggests that in the future British universities limit their higher offices to those who have taken such a course. "While such a staff college would not solve all problems," Parkinson argues, "it would provide some means of distinguishing between the able man and the windbag."[33]

The role of the vice-chancellor in the Australian universities was recently subjected to a scathing review by A. P. Rowe, former Vice-Chancellor of the University of Adelaide. Writing of his experiences in this post, Rowe clearly spells out the limitations under which the Australian vice-chancellor commonly works:

> It might be expected that after ten years as Vice-Chancellor of an Australian university I should be able to describe the powers pertaining to that office. This is not so. Indeed, it is no great exaggeration to say that an Australian vice-chancellor has no authority at all and this is perhaps one reason why I found my colleagues on the Vice-Chancellors' Committee a likeable but not very happy body of men. Moreover, in an Australian university, discussion of the powers of a vice-chancellor is not encouraged and those who might contribute to a solution of the mystery shelter behind clichés such as *primus inter pares* and control by persuasion. *Primus inter pares:* but in what way a vice-chancellor is equal to his professorial colleagues I never discovered.[34]

Arguing that the vice-chancellor should be concerned with the university as a whole and not with the internal affairs of the individual departments, Rowe

[28] The Robbins Report, pp. 221–22; and Pauline Tompkins, "Australian Higher Education and the Murray Report," *Journal of Higher Education*, Vol. 29 (October, 1958), p. 368.

[29] The Robbins Report, p. 221.

[30] *Ibid.*

[31] *Ibid.*

[32] C. Northcote Parkinson, "Organization and Method," *Universities Review*, Vol. 32 (October, 1959), p. 12.

[33] *Ibid.*, p. 13.

[34] Rowe, *If The Gown Fits*, p. 27.

scores "what in my view are the two greatest evils in the kind of university of which I write: a departmentalism which tends to make a university into a number of isolated units, and an egalitarianism which assumes that all departments and all professors are equally worthy of support."[35] The former vice-chancellor, after criticizing the lack of central control over academic policy and internal communications, concludes by saying, "Within my experience of administration I have found nothing so absurd as the position of an Australian university vice-chancellor. Those who would have him remain powerless and therefore harmless to the able and idle alike, will talk of control by persuasion. No organization works in this way, not even a monastery; and it certainly does not suffice for a university which spends annually a million pounds or more of public money."[36]

As a remedy for this situation Rowe suggests the creation in Australian universities of a committee of long-term or permanent deans, each the head of a separate faculty, under the chairmanship of the vice-chancellor. This cabinet-like committee would be authorized to decide all policies affecting teaching and research in the university, including the allocation of funds to the academic departments. Each dean would supervise closely the affairs of his own faculty and would report directly to the vice-chancellor. The aim of this arrangement would be to reduce the number of faculty committees, the work of which Rowe considers detrimental to teaching and research. A separate finance committee, composed equally of lay members of the governing body and selected deans, would be responsible for raising funds for the university and deciding upon its allocation between "the academic, administrative, and maintenance" functions of the university.[37]

In several European countries the strengthening of the rector's office represents an important step in a general policy of allowing universities more autonomy in administrative matters. Undoubtedly the growth in university enrollment has made it much more difficult than in the past to administer institutions of higher education from a central Ministry of Education. In the Netherlands, for example, the Higher Education Act of 1961 not only gives greater authority to the rector, but in addition permits the state universities and the municipal university of Amsterdam to become corporate bodies with the right to receive grants-in-aid from the state without precise prescription for its use.[38] In West Germany similar changes are taking place. Thus at the Universities of Cologne, Frankfurt, Giessen, the Free University of Berlin, and the Technical University of Berlin the nonacademic administration has been entrusted to a *Kuratorium*, a governing board drawing its membership from the academic profession and the community in which the university is situated. In the Free University of Berlin this governing board appoints a *Kurator* to carry out its directives, rather than leaving these tasks to a representative of the local education authorities.

In appraising these new approaches to university management in West Germany, some well-placed observers have raised doubts about the power

[35] *Ibid.*, p. 28.

[36] *Ibid.*, pp. 28–29.

[37] *Ibid.*, pp. 210–14. Some writers would contest Rowe's observations, maintaining that in fact the role of the vice-chancellor is already quite strong and does not need more boosting. See Pauline Tompkins, "University Education in Australia and New Zealand—Some Observations," *The Educational Record*, Vol. 40 (April, 1959), p. 163.

[38] The Robbins Report, Appendix Five, p. 108.

which may be inadvertently placed in the office of the *Kurator*. By virtue of his longer tenure and greater immediate access to vital information, this official may be able to amass considerably more influence over the members of a governing board than the *Rektor* or other academic representatives, even on subjects normally deemed "academic," such as the establishment of new teaching positions. It has also been argued that the intervention of a board representing both the academic staff and the public may itself turn out to be a hindrance to efficient management.[39]

While the drift in higher education on the Continent has been toward greater freedom from state control, somewhat the opposite trend has occurred in the British Commonwealth. Here university autonomy has appeared to be threatened by an emerging pattern of state financial support. In Great Britain the growing dependence of the universities upon government grants for salaries, capital development, and research has precipitated widespread fears that financial solvency will be achieved only at the expense of the traditional right of the universities to govern themselves. One observer, Professor Simmons of Leicester University, has warned that "the dangers of state control are real, and obvious to any one who looks, for instance, at the history of the German universities in the 1930's. These dangers, in a milder and more insidious form, may be nearer in Britain than most people suppose."[40] Simmons is particularly incensed over the attempts by the University Grants Committee to adopt "standard tests of comparison," such as "cost per student place" in building halls of residence, and in other areas of university life as well. The result of these standard tests, however well meant, unfortunately lead to what Simmons has termed the "worship of economy," a charge not unknown in many American state universities. Still another commentator, in responding to the government view that "a closer control over the spending of the [universities'] non-recurrent grants is desirable,"[41] argued: "Make them answerable to bureaucracy for every penny of government grant, and originality and creative thought will be endangered. . . . It is far better that the taxpayer should lose one or two million pounds by inefficiency than waste far more through misplaced curiosity."[42]

Despite these fears, there is little evidence that the British government has gone very far in "interfering" with its universities up to this point. Most observers agree that the government has shown considerable restraint in its dealings with institutions of higher education, particularly in view of the precarious state of the British economy during the past decade. But what the future will hold remains to be seen.

The Australian Universities Commission was established in 1959 with the two basic functions of recommending to the Commonwealth government "the sums of money needed to sustain the universities and of attempting some

[39] Hahn, "Patterns and Trends in West German Universities," p. 251.

[40] Jack Simmons, *New University* (Leicester, Eng.: Leicester University Press, 1959), p. 202.

[41] *Fifth Report from the Select Committee on Estimates* (*1951–52*), paragraph 37, quoted in Simmons, *New University*, p. 200.

[42] *Economist*, August 26, 1950, quoted in Simmons, *New University*, p. 200. For similar comment see Stephen Toulmin, "Financing the Universities," *The Spectator*, March 30, 1962, p. 394; the Robbins Report, Evidence—Part One (Vol. F), memorandum and testimony given by Professor Ely Devons, pp. 1772–74, 1779–89.

coordination of university development."[43] Generally this action does not appear to have stirred up, as yet, anything resembling the controversy over university-state relations in Great Britain. As one writer has put it: "It would appear that university teachers felt that they would be in a better position if they worked under the aegis of the Commonwealth and the spectacle of unending research grants, and a status akin to that of the Australian public servant has blinded them to the dangers of total Commonwealth controls."[44] Whether the situation will remain unchanged in years to come is another question. As dependence upon Commonwealth subsidies continues to mount, it appears reasonable to expect that voices will increasingly be raised demanding greater information on how public funds are being spent.

One of the major changes that has occurred in recent years in European and Commonwealth universities is a weakening of the traditional practice of leaving university government in the hands of committees made up of senior faculty members only. The postwar boom in student enrollments has imposed so heavy a burden of administration upon senior academicians that they have found it increasingly difficult to carry on their normal teaching and research responsibilities. P. H. Partridge has best summed up this dilemma for Australian universities:

> Within universities there are certain problems which we are dishonest in our refusal to face. . . . The hypocrisy is that we continue to pretend that administration is something extra that the professor takes in his stride, while he continues to be essentially a teacher and a scholar. . . . We should be more honest if we would admit that, in many university departments and faculties, administration is now a separate and important function, and that there is often enough of it to provide full-time employment for one or more men. We may be right in our suspicion of introducing professional administrators into our universities; we may be right in holding to the view that academic administration should be done by people who have been academics. But we are probably getting the worst of all possible worlds by producing a race of part-time teachers, part-time scholars, part-time administrators. . . . whatever gives under the strain, it is usually not the administrative duties.[45]

In Great Britain the professors "complain bitterly about the number of administrative duties thrown upon them and also about the time they are compelled to waste as members of an unconscionable number of committees."[46] A similar situation may be said to prevail in most Continental universities. Thus the West German Conference of *Rektors*, in a move unusual for a body representing academic self-government, recently "stressed emphatically the state's responsibility either to furnish the universities with additional administrative personnel . . . or to strengthen the departments of university administration in the ministries of education."[47]

A solution to this problem has been sought in a variety of directions. Most common has been the demand that the senior academicians turn over some of

[43] The Robbins Report, Appendix Five, p. 39.

[44] Stewart Fraser, "Recent Developments in Australian Higher Education," *Comparative Education Review*, Vol. 5 (June, 1961), p. 33.

[45] P. H. Partridge, "The State of the Universities," in *Melbourne Studies in Education* (London: Cambridge University Press, 1962), pp. 91–92.

[46] "Notes," *Universities Review*, Vol. 33 (October, 1960), p. 4.

[47] Hahn, "Patterns and Trends in West German Universities," p. 253.

their responsibilities to younger men on the faculty. In Great Britain one review has stated: "The solution of this problem does not lie in giving greater power to the administrator but in a wider distribution of responsibility among the members of the teaching staff. If this were to be done, the present unrest among lecturers would be largely dissipated for they would then feel that they had been fully absorbed into the life of the university . . . if this division of responsibility and work took place the professor would then have more time to devote to his research and teaching."[48] The Robbins Committee, in recommending that junior faculty members be allowed to play a full part in academic self-government, noted that, "like any other machinery, the machinery for the academic government of a university can only work efficiently if it is not overloaded."[49] And there is strong evidence, at least in the newer universities in Great Britain, that junior members of the teaching staff are indeed being asked to play a more important role in internal decision making.[50]

In West Germany proposals along the same line have called for senior professors to delegate "a good deal" of authority to a small executive committee of each faculty. Another means of relieving professors of some of their administrative burdens is to restrict administrative duties to staff members below the rank of full professor. This approach has been contemplated for a new university to be established in Konstanz.[51] It is also possible to decentralize administrative authority to the individual faculties, laying stress on the decision-making potential of each academic department. This approach has been favored in France, with each department under a separate head whose responsibilities have been defined so as to relieve the dean of the faculty of much of his day-to-day responsibility.[52]

Moving in the opposite direction, several universities in different countries have taken steps to build up the duties of such administrative officers as registrars and bursars. In Australia the development of these offices, particularly the role of the registrar, has gone so far in recent years that one observer has argued "that university administration as a career, with the post of registrar as ultimate goal, is well established."[53] Perhaps the clearest support for transferring administrative responsibility from faculty to full-time administrators has come from Albert E. Sloman, Vice-Chancellor of the new University of Essex in Great Britain:

> we intend . . . to follow the lead of one or two of the biggest universities in this country and build up under the registrar a strong secretariat, some of whom will work with deans of schools and, when they are big, with departments. We shall do everything in our power to remove routine administrative work from academic staff so as to leave them time for teaching and research, time also for really stra-

[48] "Notes."

[49] The Robbins Report, p. 220.

[50] Albert E. Sloman, *A University in the Making* (New York: Oxford University Press, 1964), p. 86. For a somewhat pessimistic view of this problem see Sir Eric Ashby, "Introduction: Decision-Making in the Academic World," in Halmos (ed.), *Sociological Studies in British University Education*, pp. 5–11.

[51] Hahn "Patterns and Trends in West German Universities," p. 252; see also Wolfgang Clemen, *Idee und Wirklichkeit auf der Universitat* (Heidelberg: Quelle and Meyer, 1963), p. 14.

[52] The Robbins Report, Appendix Five, p. 68.

[53] Tompkins, "University Education in Australia and New Zealand," p. 163.

tegic thinking on policy. We recognize also that universities will need trained administrators if they are to be efficiently run. All the different branches of university administration, whether estates and planning, or finance, or academic business, require nowadays specialized skills and techniques. Nationally there is a need also for more systematic and standardized records, of both students and staff. With its variety of interest, its responsibility, and its scope for promotion, university administration is a career, I believe, which will rapidly increase in importance. It is a sort of academic civil service.[54]

In Great Britain there have even been signs that institutional research is becoming an accepted and necessary part of university administration, although progress in this area, as in others, has been slow. All but three British universities recently participated in a study of applicants to universities conducted for the Committee of Vice-Chancellors and Principals. The Institution of Education in London has now set up a research unit on student problems, and Sloman has proposed the establishment at the University of Essex of a unit for research into higher education. "The unit will be concerned first with the university's own problems of planning and organization. It will document its experiments in courses of study, in the use of discussion classes, in study-rooms for students living outside the university, in fact the whole of its social and intellectual life."[55]

Needless to say, none of these portents of change presages any rush on the part of European and Commonwealth universities to adopt American innovations in university management in their entirety. There has been and continues to be strong resistance against any move which might dilute academic authority in these institutions. Moreover, in Europe as in America, there is a profound fear that rationalized management will undermine traditional academic values. But, as Sir Eric Ashby says of British academicians, "All over the country these groups of scholars, who would not make a decision about the shape of a leaf or the derivation of a word or the author of a manuscript without painstakingly assembling the evidence, make decisions about admissions policy, size of universities, staff-student ratios, content of courses, and similar issues, based on dubious assumptions, scrappy data, and mere hunch . . . although dedicated to the pursuit of knowledge, they have until recently resolutely declined to pursue knowledge about themselves."[56]

Despite this kind of resistance, changes in university administration can certainly be expected to occur at an ever-increasing rate in the universities of Europe and the British Commonwealth. At institutions on the Continent, for example, it will become increasingly difficult for important administrative decisions affecting higher education to be made in a central government agency. This will lead to more and more authority being delegated to universities themselves, and particularly to the office of the rector and his assistants. The administrative organization of institutions of higher education abroad will change because the urgency of the times requires such transformation. Practices developed at a time when universities were small and management duties few cannot continue unchanged when these institutions have become immense and their tasks of administration overwhelming.

[54] Sloman, *A University in the Making*, pp. 86–87.

[55] *Ibid.*, pp. 85–86. See also "Studying Higher Education in Britain and America," *Universities Quarterly*, Vol. 17 (March, 1963), pp. 126–48; and Ashby, "Introduction: Decision-Making in the Academic World," p. 6.

[56] Ashby, "Introduction: Decision-Making in the Academic World," p. 6.

SOURCES TO TABLES C–1 AND C–3, BY COUNTRY AND YEAR

Country	Year	Source
Great Britain	1949/50	*Report of the Committee on Higher Education: Appendix Two (A)—Students and Their Education* (London: H.M. Stationery Office, 1963), Table 1, p. 17. Hereafter this will be referred to as the Robbins Report, with the appendix, where used, appropriately cited.
	1953/54	*Ibid.*, Table 3, p. 19; *Commonwealth Universities Yearbook* (1956).
	1959/60	See 1949/50.
	1963/64	See 1953/54; *The Statesman's Yearbook* (1964/65), p. 80.
	1970/71	The Robbins Report, Chart E, p. 161.
Australia	1949/50	*Commonwealth Universities Yearbook* (1949–50).
	1953/54	*Ibid.* (1955).
	1959/60	The Robbins Report, Appendix Five, Table I.5, p. 251.
	1963/64	*Yearbook of the Commonwealth of Australia*, No. 50 (1964), p. 732.
	1970/71	See 1959/60.
Canada	1949/50	*The Statesman's Yearbook* (1952), p. 350.
	1959/60	The Robbins Report, Appendix Five, Table J.2, p. 253.
	1963/64	*The Europa Year Book* (1965), Vol. II, p. 225.
	1970/71	The Robbins Report, Appendix Five, Table J.5, p. 255.
France	1949/50	The Robbins Report, Appendix Five, Table K.3, p. 257.
	1959/60	See 1949/50.
	1953/54	*The Statesman's Yearbook* (1956), p. 972.
	1963/64	Table 1 figure calculated on the basis of the rate of growth of the two previous years, as presented in *Education in France*, published by the Cultural Services of the French Embassy, No. 28 (June, 1965), Table IV, p. 8. Table 2 figure taken from *The World of Learning* (1964–65), pp. 353–77, and *Education in France.*
	1970/71	The Robbins Report, Appendix Five, p. 73.
West Germany	1949/50	*Statistisches Jahrbuch fur die Bundesrepublik Deutschland* (1953), pp. 94–95.
	1953/54	*Ibid.* (1955), pp. 92–93.
	1959–60	*Ibid.* (1962), pp. 103–4.
	1963/64	*Ibid.* (1964), pp. 102–3.
	1970/71	Friedrich Edding, "The University Enrollment in West Germany," *Comparative Education Review*, Vol. 9 (February, 1965), p. 9.
Netherlands	1949/50	*The Statesman's Yearbook* (1951), p. 1252.
	1953/54	*Ibid.* (1955), p. 1237, and *The World of Learning* (1954), pp. 582–90.
	1959/60	The Robbins Report, Appendix Five, Table N.1, p. 264.
	1963/64	*The World of Learning* (1964/65), pp. 826–38.
	1970/71	See 1959/60.
Italy	1949/50	*Annuario Statistico Italiano* (1951), Table 87, p. 99.
	1953/54	*The Statesman's Yearbook* (1957), p. 1165.
	1959/60	*Annuario Statistico Italiano* (1961), Table 109, p. 111.
	1962/63	*Compendio Statistico Italiano* (1964), Table 69, p. 73.

Sweden	1949/50	Approximate calculation from data in *The Statesman's Yearbook* (1951), p. 1391, based on the definition of higher education presented in The Robbins Report, Appendix Five, Table 1, p. 140.
	1953/54	The Robbins Report, Appendix Five, Table 1, p. 140; *Statistical Abstract of Sweden* (1961), Table 328, p. 266. *The Statesman's Yearbook* (1955), pp. 1375–1376.
	1959/60	The Robbins Report, Appendix Five, Table P.1, p. 269.
	1963/64	*The World of Learning* (1964/65), pp. 1020–27; *The Statesman's Yearbook* (1964/65), p. 1432.
	1970/71	The Robbins Report, Appendix Five, p. 144.
Switzerland	1949/50	*Statistisches Jahrbuch der Schweiz* (1953), p. 465.
	1953/54	*Ibid.*, pp. 463, 472, 474.
	1959/60	*Ibid.* (1959/60), pp. 462, 470, 472.
	1963/64	*Ibid.* (1964), pp. 459, 467, 469.
United States	1949/50	*Digest of Educational Statistics*, Office of Education, No. 18 (Washington: U.S. Government Printing Office, 1964), Table 51, p. 74.
	1953/54	See 1949/50.
	1954/55	Office of Education, *Education Directory: 1954–55, Part3, Higher Education* (Washington: U.S. Government Printing Office, 1955).
	1959/60	See 1949/50.
	1963/64	See 1949/50.
	1964/65	Office of Education, *Education Directory: 1964–65, Part 3, Higher Education* (Washington: U.S. Government Printing Office, 1965).
	1970/71	The Robbins Report, Appendix Five, p. 175.

SELECTED BIBLIOGRAPHY

Up to this time the literature which bears directly on the managerial innovations we have been investigating is not plentiful. The most relevant material available can be found in the various proceedings of workshops and conferences held in recent years on institutional research and other aspects of academic administration. These meetings were sponsored for the most part by the regional associations in which public institutions of higher education have increasingly come to be grouped, and we would certainly recommend that readers interested in the topics we have examined in previous chapters consult the published proceedings of such conferences, a number of which are listed in this bibliography.

In drawing up the general scheme of our analysis, we have also relied very heavily on the literature that has emerged since World War II in the field of organization theory. To the extent that organization theory has an empirical basis, much of this literature rests on the experience of hierarchical organizations —factories, industrial firms, and the like. It thus assumes a chain of command in which authority flows from the top to the bottom. Needless to say, the operation of institutions of higher education does not correspond to any such model. As indicated in Chapter 1, academic institutions rather belong in the category of professional organizations—in which the basis of authority is knowledge rather than hierarchical rank and in which power over decision does not, therefore, correspond with status in the hierarchy. But there are a number of writers in the field of organization theory whose work does throw the distinctive features of professional organizations into sharp relief, and this literature has been very valuable to us in our research.

Some of the items listed in the bibliography describe the development of academic administration outside the United States—a subject discussed in Appendix C. For other bibliographic references in the field of comparative university administration, the reader is referred to the footnotes in Appendix C. We have also included a number of items from the general literature of higher education which do not deal directly with academic administration, but which have been very useful to us in framing the setting for our study, or in enabling us to gain a broader perspective on our materials. Certainly nothing is more important to an understanding of the organization and administration of institutions of higher education than an awareness of the fundamental human purposes which such institutions seek to achieve or even to embody. For example, the extreme dispersion of authority, which is the university's prime organizational characteristic, mirrors the commitment in the academic community to the independence of the individual scholar.

Bagley, Clarence H. *A Conceptual Framework for Institutional Research.* Pullman, Wash.: Office of Institutional Research, Washington State University, 1964.

Braybrooke, David, and Charles E. Lindblom. *A Strategy of Decision.* New York: The Free Press of Glencoe, 1963.

Brumbaugh, A. J. *Research Designed to Improve Institutions of Higher Learning.* Washington: American Council on Education, 1960.

Burns, Gerald P. (ed.). *Administrators in Higher Education: Their Functions and Coordination.* New York: Harper and Row, 1962.

Callahan, Raymond E. *Education and the Cult of Efficiency.* Chicago: University of Chicago Press, 1962.

Caplow, Theodore, and Reece J. McGee. *The Academic Marketplace.* New York: Basic Books, 1958.

Castelpoggi, Raymond (ed.). *Academic Effectiveness.* Amherst: University of Massachusetts, 1964.

Clark, Burton R. "Organizational Adaptation and Precarious Values: A Case Study," *American Sociological Review,* Vol. 21 (June, 1956), pp. 327–36.

———. "Faculty Authority," *AAUP Bulletin,* Vol. 47 (December, 1961), pp. 293–302.

Conference on Institutional Research in Higher Education. Research Bulletin No. 6. DeKalb, Ill.: Northern Illinois University, 1962.

Corson, John J. *Governance of Colleges and Universities.* New York: McGraw-Hill, 1960.

Dodds, Harold W. *The Academic President—Educator or Caretaker?* New York: McGraw-Hill, 1962.

Duryea, E. D. *Management of Learning.* Washington: U.S. Office of Education, 1960.

Enarson, H. L. "Innovation in Higher Education," *Journal of Higher Education,* Vol. 31 (December, 1960), pp. 495–501.

Etzioni, Amitai. "Authority Structure and Organizational Effectiveness," *Administrative Science Quarterly,* Vol. 4 (June, 1959), pp. 43–67.

———. *A Comparative Analysis of Complex Organizations.* New York: The Free Press of Glencoe, 1961.

———. *Modern Organizations.* Englewood Cliffs, N.J.: Prentice-Hall, 1964.

Goodman, Paul. *The Community of Scholars.* New York: Random House, 1962.

Griffiths, Daniel E. (ed.). *Behavioral Science and Educational Administration, The Sixty-third Yearbook of the National Society for the Study of Education.* Part II. Chicago: National Society for the Study of Education, 1964.

Gross, Bertram M. *The Managing of Organizations: The Administrative Struggle.* 2 vols. New York: The Free Press of Glencoe, 1964.

Hallenbeck, Edwin F., and Leo F. Redfern. *A College Colloquium on Institutional Research.* Kingston: University of Rhode Island, 1962.

Halmos, Paul (ed.). *Sociological Studies in British University Education.* Monograph No. 7 of *The Sociological Review.* Keele: University of Keele, 1963.

Hearle, Edward F. R. "How Useful are 'Scientific' Tools of Management?" *Public Administration Review,* Vol. 21 (Autumn, 1961), pp. 206–9.

Hofstadter, Richard, and C. DeWitt Hardy. *The Development and Scope of Higher Education in the United States.* New York: Columbia University Press, 1952.

Hofstadter, Richard, and Walter P. Metzger. *The Development of Academic Freedom in the United States.* New York: Columbia University Press, 1955.

Howell, Charles E., and Milton E. Carlson. *Institutional Research.* DeKalb, Ill.: Northern Illinois University, 1961.

Kerr, Clark. *The Uses of the University*. Cambridge: Harvard University Press, 1963.

Knorr, Owen A. (ed.). *Long-Range Planning in Higher Education*. Boulder, Colo.: Western Interstate Commission for Higher Education, April, 1965.

Leavitt, Harold J. "Unhuman Organizations," *Harvard Business Review*, Vol. 40 (July–August, 1962), pp. 90–98.

Lindblom, Charles E. "The Science of 'Muddling Through'," *Public Administration Review*, Vol. 19 (Spring, 1959), pp. 79–88.

Lins, L. Joseph (ed.). *Basis for Decision*. Madison, Wis.: Dembar Educational Research Services, Inc., 1963.

——— (ed.). *The Role of Institutional Research in Planning*. Madison: Office of Institutional Studies, University of Wisconsin, 1963.

Lunsford, Terry F. (ed.). *The Study of Academic Administration*. Boulder, Colo.: Western Interstate Commission for Higher Education, 1963.

March, James G. (ed.). *Handbook of Organizations*. Chicago: Rand McNally, 1965.

March, James G., and Herbert A. Simon. *Organizations*. New York: John Wiley, 1958.

Miles, E. P., and D. L. Hartford. *A Study of Administrative Uses of Computers in Colleges and Universities of the United States*. Tallahassee: Florida State University, 1962.

Miller, James L., Jr. *State Budgeting for Higher Education*. Ann Arbor: Institute of Public Administration, University of Michigan, 1964.

Millett, John D. *The Academic Community: An Essay on Organization*. New York: McGraw-Hill, 1962.

Moos, Malcolm, and Francis E. Rourke. *The Campus and the State*. Baltimore: The Johns Hopkins Press, 1959.

Perkins, James A. *The University in Transition*. Princeton, N.J.: Princeton University Press, 1966.

Redfern, Leo F. "The Calculating Administrators: Experience with Electronic Computers at the University of Massachusetts," *State Government*, Vol. 36 (Summer, 1963), pp. 183–88.

Report of the Committee on Higher Education. London: H.M. Stationery Office, 1963. Generally referred to as the Robbins Report.

Riesman, David. *Constraint and Variety in American Education*. Lincoln: University of Nebraska Press, 1956.

Rourke, Francis E. "Bureaucracy in Conflict: Administrators and Professionals," *Ethics*, LXX (April, 1960), 220–27.

Rudolph, Frederick. *The American College and University*. New York: Alfred A. Knopf, 1962.

Russell, John Dale. "Changing Patterns of Administrative Organization in Higher Education," *Annals* of the American Academy of Political and Social Science, Vol. 301 (September, 1955), pp. 22–31.

Sanford, Nevitt. *The American College*. New York: John Wiley, 1962.

Selznick, Philip. *Leadership in Administration*. Evanston, Ill.: Row, Peterson, 1957.

Shultz, George P., and Thomas L. Whisler (eds.). *Management Organization and the Computer*. New York: The Free Press of Glencoe, 1960.

Simon, Herbert A. *The New Science of Management Decision*. New York: Harper and Row, 1960.

Sloman, Albert E. *A University in the Making*. New York: Oxford University Press, 1964.

Sprague, Hall T. *Institutional Research in the West*. Boulder, Colo.: Western Interstate Commission for Higher Education, 1960.

Stickler, W. Hugh. *Institutional Research Concerning Land Grant Institutions and State Universities*. Tallahassee: Office of Institutional Research and Service, Florida State University, 1959.

Thompson, Victor. *Modern Organization: A General Theory*. New York: Alfred A. Knopf, 1961.

Western Interstate Commission for Higher Education. *Studies of College Faculty*. Boulder, Colo.: WICHE, 1961.

Wildavsky, Aaron. *The Politics of the Budgetary Process*. Boston: Little, Brown, 1964.

Williams, Harry. *Planning for Effective Resource Allocation in Universities*. Washington: American Council on Education, 1966.

Wilson, Logan. *Academic Man*. New York: Oxford University Press, 1942.

——— (ed.). *Emerging Patterns in American Higher Education*. Washington: American Council on Education, 1965.

INDEX

The Managerial Revolution in Higher Education
by
Francis E. Rourke and Glenn E. Brooks

designer: Gerard A. Valerio
typesetter: Baltimore Type and Composition Corporation
typefaces: 10/12 Times Roman Text; Goudy Handtooled Display
printer: Maple Press
paper: 60 lb. Mohawk Tosca Book
binder: Moore and Company, Inc.
cover material: Columbia Riverside Linen, RL-1958